NO WAY

Robert Moore

Fulton Books
Meadville, PA

Published by Fulton Books 2022

ISBN 978-1-63860-274-3 (paperback)
ISBN 978-1-63860-275-0 (digital)

Printed in the United States of America

First of all, I dedicate this book to *our Father* who is in heaven watching us, listening to every word we say and think. I want to dedicate this book to our Father for sending His only Son, Jesus Christ, to be beaten, tortured, and made fun of so that when He died for us—His children—we could be forgiven for our sins and rise from the dead so that we too could join Him in heaven where there is always light and never dark.

I also dedicate this book to the *Holy Spirit* who has been there to persuade us to do good and to find our Father's Son, Jesus Christ.

I want to dedicate this book to *Jesus Christ* for allowing me to be able to use His name to tell Satan to get behind me when sin comes into my mind.

I want to dedicate this book to my blood family for not giving up on me, even though I know that they wanted to but still stood there waiting for the day that I beat this drug addiction.

I dedicate this book to my three children (babies) that they may not go down the same road that I went down.

I dedicate this book to my loving preacher Tony White and his loving wife Flo for all the prayers for me and the loving family that I have at Brickyard Road Baptist Church in Powell, Tennessee.

I want to dedicate this book to all who are still in the world, walking in darkness, that they too may find the light where the truth is and freedom from darkness.

I dedicate this book to the one who knows the truth but still has problems grasping it.

I dedicate this book to all the addicts who have quit, are trying to quit, the ones still using, and the ones picking up for the first time for they do not know the road ahead—a trap leading to a dead end that is six feet deep, death!

I dedicate this book to my loving sister in Christ who has been with me since those last couple of weeks at rehab, who I met at church, and who I talk to almost every day—Sue Piro. Thanks for all your help and guidance. I love you so much. Thanks!

I dedicate this book to my dear friends Larry and his loving wife Wanda who have tried to help me throughout the years and for giving me work to do around their house.

I also dedicate this book to all the rehabs and facilities that devote their time to helping others with addiction, mental illness, etc.

I dedicate this book to all the people who preach, teach, and spread the truth, the light—an answer to salvation!

I dedicate this book to all the children who grow up not knowing the truth, may you find the truth. And for the ones who do know the truth, may all of you accept the truth, the tight, the best shepherd, the one true way to salvation, Jesus Christ.

I dedicate the proceeds of this book: the first 10 percent goes to our Father, God. After paying bills and other debts, my goal is to open up a facility to help people with addictions and show them how they have been lied to, walking around with a blindfold in the dark. Then I want to share with them the love, the light, and the truth, our Savior and King of kings, Jesus Christ. Our Father God gave Him authority overall, and He sits at our Father's right hand, wearing the crown of crowns for Jesus is the key to eternity.

This dedication goes out to the world. I pray that you may find the truth, the light, the best shepherd, Jesus Christ. All our lives, God, our Father who is in Heaven, has asked one thing of us during this time we spend on earth—to believe, trust, have faith, and truly accept His only Son into our hearts. I ask you today that if you are walking around with a blindfold being lied to, please, for the love of God, talk to Him. Tell Him you need help and understanding, and tell Him you want the light that leads to the truth, Jesus Christ. When you do this, have faith that what you say is being heard, and make sure it comes from the heart! Remember, God gave us the key—Jesus Christ, the answer to what God asks of us. I tell you that if or when you accept Jesus Christ, you will love it. As for me, I'm sorry that I didn't do this when I was younger because it is so beautiful!

INTRODUCTION

This book that I have written is for the world and for us who are in the world. I hope it opens gates in your mind that offer answers to any questions that you may have. Even as I sit here, I know that I have found the answer to *life*: it is the truth, the light. In this book, I say many times that what I tell you is God's honest truth. This story is no exaggeration of what went on in my life and what I saw and did. During this time, I was lost in total darkness, blind to the truth.

As you read this book, I know that there are many people who have seen, heard, and experienced the exact same thing that I did, and I want to share answers as to what I believe it all was and why. I give many quotes, and still to this day, I know that they are 99 percent correct (if not, 100 percent). The people that I talk to look at me and say, "How did you know that?" and, "I just thought that it was the drug!" Some even know what it is and just go on with life battling their addiction, looking for a way out. But for me, *no*! For I am at war. I know the truth, and I am in the light!

Over the years, I asked people lots of questions, but all I found were incorrect answers. I didn't start getting real answers until I found myself in jail. That's when the Lord spoke to me and set me straight. Then in rehab, by reading the Bible, the Lord would let me know the answers to the questions I was looking for, even when I was just reading.

In this book, I say, "*No way!*" a lot. "No way, this is not possible!" But let me tell you, there is a way, and it is possible. Today, as I write this, I wonder if I will ever again say, "No way," because "no way" has a completely new meaning to me now!

FORGIVENESS

I want everyone to know that no matter what happened in the past, even growing up, I offer my forgiveness. I will also forgive anyone and everyone who may do anything in the future. I will turn the other cheek because I believe God will take care of it.

One more thing: if you don't forgive, then remember, it's in our Father's hands. Do you really want to leave it up to Him?

PROLOGUE

My name is Robert T. Moore IV. I was born at 12:16 a.m. on November 9, 1967, at Baptist Hospital in Knoxville, Tennessee. I had a great childhood—played in the mud, climbed trees, caught bugs, and played ball.

I was raised in church. At a young age, my mom approached me and asked if I would like to be saved. I really didn't understand what that meant; I just knew that I wanted to go to heaven. So my sister, who was about four and a half years older than me, and I approached the preacher together and announced Jesus Christ as our Savior.

No sooner had I accepted Him as my Savior when I kept hearing a blasting sound in my ears. I couldn't understand what was going on. Why wouldn't it stop? After a time, it would go away, and I would forget about it. But when I would forget, it would start back over—over and over again. I'm not sure exactly when it stopped for good, but it did. Today, looking back, I can honestly say, "That was not me" (Ephesians 6:12 explains).

At around age seven or so, my dad and I were in the front yard at our house, and he began to warn me about drugs. When he was done, I couldn't understand what *high* meant. What did he mean by "get high"? I also couldn't understand how something like that could control a person. Though I know he meant well, my dad's warning made me feel confused.

By the time I was eleven or twelve years old, I was dipping tobacco; soon after that, I was smoking cigarettes. By the age of seventeen, I was drinking alcohol and smoking pot. At age eighteen, I bought my first bag of pot. Around the age of twenty-four, I was using cocaine and, shortly after that, began smoking crack. That's when all the things my dad had said about drugs controlling a person came into play.

I was doing whatever I could to make money. I needed money because I needed crack. I went through a couple of years doing pills, and at times, I was even snorting them. Then meth came into the picture, and that's when I started using a needle. I knew I had a problem, but to be truthful, I don't even know if I cared. I spent four years doing meth/ice, and then it happened—I got arrested.

You may think that's the end, but for me, it was just the beginning. I heard God's voice four times, and that was when I started following Jesus. This is my story.

CHAPTER 1

My story begins about the time I was forty-four years old. I had been clean about a year—except drinking. So technically, I was not clean. I believed that since I was not using drugs, I was clean. But really, all that means is that I was blind and in denial.

On Halloween, I met this beautiful young woman named Sharon, seventeen years younger than I was. We struck up a conversation, and the whole time, I was in awe, thinking, *I cannot believe that she is talking to me!* As we talked, we discovered that we had a lot in common: we both had been on drugs, we liked to drink, and we were both going through a divorce. When I decided to leave later that night, I got her phone number.

Before I knew it, we were in a relationship, and it was going great.

We hadn't been together too long when Sharon told me she wanted a pill, not realizing that pills were her drug of choice; I was completely against it. Eventually, though, I gave in and got her one. The next thing I knew, she expected one every day.

My girlfriend became a full-blown addict. When she would do a pill, it was like she never, ever quit running her mouth. I could not get a word in, no matter how hard I tried, and I was always wrong. Still, it got to where I would sometimes do a pill with her.

Not long after, Sharon asked me, "Have you ever done meth?"

"No, and I never will," I blurted.

The next thing I knew, I was taking her to get meth. When we got back to my house with the drugs, she announced, "I'm not doing this by myself."

I didn't want to try it, but after about an hour, I gave in, and she was happy.

As we got deeper into meth, I began to see strange things. It all started with Sharon's skin—it looked like her face and legs had been burnt, almost as if she was scarred from being burned by fire. There would be times it looked like she had red sores (dots) on her face. I would sit there and shake my head and try to adjust my eyes. I would tell her what I was seeing, and she would just tell me, "You was tripping!"

In spite of these strange appearances, life was getting more exciting, and I was falling deeper and deeper in love. Some nights, Sharon would dance in front of the mirror for hours, sometimes all night. There were times we'd talk all night surrounded by candles. The thing about meth was that I was finally able to get two cents in and sometimes a nickel of conversation. Sharon even went so far as to make up "rules" for how long she would talk so that I could have a turn.

This didn't stop the strange things from appearing, though. In fact, they started to take on different forms. When Sharon and I were together in bed doing our thing, it seemed like another woman appeared, but then she'd be gone, and it was just Sharon there. She would leave the room, come back, and she would be another woman.

I finally questioned, "Where did Sharon go?"

My girlfriend thought that I was playing with her, so she answered, "She's here somewhere, she didn't leave."

I looked around for her and went to the front door, looked out the peephole, and there was Sharon's car. Turning back to her, I reasoned, "She is here somewhere because her car is still outside." Then I came to the realization that it was Sharon the whole time.

When I asked her about it, she admitted, "I thought that you were playing with me, so I played along with you."

More things started to unfold. One night, on our way home from getting some meth, I was feeling hungry. The whole time, Sharon kept messing with the meth in the car. I finally warned, "Quit playing with it or you're going to spill it!"

When we got home, I acted as if I was getting out of the car, but when Sharon got out, I took off. I called her and asked her what she wanted. She told me to come back and get her. I asked her if she would leave the dope at the house, and she said no. So I explained that I had already left and wasn't coming back until I got something for us to eat. I went to a drive-through, got our order, and began eating.

When I pulled up in the driveway at my house, I started looking in my rearview mirror at a nearby house where a policeman lived. The next thing I knew, I was waking up.

My girlfriend came outside and demanded, "Where have you been?" She explained that she had been trying to get ahold of me for about two hours. I was in shock, wondering how I had been out that long and how I managed to fall asleep like I did.

We went inside where I fell into bed and immediately went back to sleep. Sharon woke me up and said, "Here, sniff some dope, and you will wake up."

"No, leave me alone."

She would not leave me alone, being very persistent and demanding.

Finally, I growled, "Get it out of my face or I will knock it out of your hands!"

Needless to say, she wouldn't stop, and I knocked it out of her hands. Meth was all over my bed. Sharon smacked me like I had never ever been slapped before.

All of a sudden, I asked her, "What are you doing here?"

"What?" she wondered, completely baffled.

I thought Sharon was my ex-wife's friend and had *no idea* that she was my girlfriend. I started grabbing clothes, and she asked, "What are you doing?"

"I'm leaving!" I announced.

"Why are you leaving?" she said. "This is your house."

I started looking around noticing things but was still confused about where I was and what was going on.

Sharon and I had gotten to know the meth dealer, Del, so I left the room and called him to ask about what was going on. He asked me, "Where is your girlfriend?" I snuck down the hall, peeked around the door, and there she was, the love of my life—my girlfriend, Sharon! I went into the room and began explaining what I thought was going on and immediately apologized for what I had done.

One night, I noticed something on the floor across the hall in the bedroom. It seemed like when I would see it, it would sneak creep around the doorjamb. It seemed as if it was playing a game with me like peekaboo. As I was trying to figure it out, Sharon said, "There's something over there on the floor. I keep seeing it move."

"I see it too," I told her.

"What is it?"

"It looks like a hand."

We both were kind of freaked out by it, so I closed the door. I thought, *Huh, funny that we both saw the same thing.*

We may have had a lot in common, but eventually, our relationship started getting bad. We were fighting over some of the most ridiculous things. I finally told Sharon I was done with the meth. When I told her that, she turned to crack cocaine. She tried to get me to smoke it with her, but I'd already been down that road and wasn't about to go down it again. Needless to say, things got worse, and *poof*—she was gone. My dream had turned into a nightmare.

CHAPTER 2

It was a day or two after New Year's, late at night, and I was drunk. My phone rang, and I didn't recognize the number. When I answered, lo and behold, it was Sharon, my ex-girlfriend.

"I told you if I ever found that stuff (meth/ice), I would call you," she stated.

Sharon asked where I was, and I told her I was at my parents' house. (My parents live just seconds from me.) She told me that she was about ten minutes away and would be right over.

When I got off the phone, I got really scared and began throwing up. I was very excited but at the same time terrified. I went upstairs to tell my mom that I was going to my house to meet someone. She begged me not to go, but I told her that everything was going to be okay.

On my way back down the stairs, I got really sick again and began throwing up. Sharon called me back and asked if I had gotten home yet. I told her that I was getting ready to leave, and she told me that her ride was about to drop her off.

When I got to my house, I couldn't believe my eyes. Sharon was really there right in front of me! It had been such a long time. I had been so much in love with her when she left, and seeing her again was like a dream come true. I can say one thing: the love I had for her was enormous and still the same, if not, bigger.

We went inside. I wasn't staying at my house at the time because my family and I had been painting the inside, and it was a mess. Still, Sharon and I went back to my room like old times and began smoking ice (meth) on aluminum foil. I was in a daze looking at her, thinking it was a dream, overwhelmed with love.

As morning approached, we realized we'd have to leave because my family would be there soon to paint the house, so we went to her place. Sharon didn't have running water because of a broken pipe, but then again, who needs running water? I was with her!

We would eventually run out of ice, hang out for a little while, do whatever, and go get some more. It was then that I met up with the dealer, Del; his girlfriend, Sarah; and one of his best friends, Little Man. I ended up calling him.

As we were getting our ice weighed out, Del was acting sketchy. *Sketchy* is a word commonly used in this way of life. To me, it means not trusting or paranoid. Del ended up asking Little Man to finish weighing it out. When we got our bag of ice, we talked very little and left. No sooner had we gotten in the car to leave when the dealer pulled up beside us. His car had been nowhere in sight, but he suddenly pulled up, still acting sketchy.

No matter how much dope we did or how long we were up only at night on ice, we could drive perfectly as long as we kept enough in our bodies. So as we drove down the road that night, my girlfriend and I started to notice something that never appeared during daylight hours. One of us would observe, "There is something in the road or crossing it." Funny that we would see the exact same thing, but it was never there.

A couple of times, we knew that we had seen a person at a distance, crossing the road, but when we got closer, there would never ever be anybody there. It got to where I would really watch them, but again—nothing. I would look across the yards in front of people's houses because the streetlights would light things up, but still, no one. Then I would look at my phone to see what time it was and wonder, *What is someone doing out at this time of night?* Then again, *we* were out, but we were in a car. Come to think of it, every time we went out at night, there always seemed to be someone out and about.

One night, we saw another person, but this one seemed different. It had the figure of a person, but it had no face, no hair, and it looked like a shadow, except pitch-black. As time went on, we would see more and more "people" like that. Depending on where they were standing dictated what color they would be. If they were around a streetlight, they would have a brown tint to them. If they weren't around a light, they would be as black as coal. They would sometimes act as if they were hiding from us but always made sure that we saw them. It was like they were playing games with us.

There would be times that these "people" would be in groups, standing in a perfect circle of twenty or thirty of them. Some would walk into the circle, while some would walk out. I wondered what they were talking about, but then it would hit me, *How can they be talking? I'm tripping, right?* But if I had just been tripping, I couldn't help but wonder, *How come Sharon and I were seeing the same thing?*

As the people left the circle, they would walk together in groups of at least six or seven. They would always cross the road in front of us; their legs visible from the light down the road. As they walked by, they would raise their hands up as if they were waving, making sure that we saw them. We, of course, would slow down and watch them, trying to figure things out.

There was this one that really sticks in my head; I often picture it to this day. This thing—whatever it was—was standing on the side of the road about fifteen feet from the car. When we were looking at it, we slowed down very slow, looking at it, and asked each other, "What is it?" I wondered, *Why is it looking at me like that?* Then the thought came across my mind, *It can't be looking at me—it doesn't have a face, and this is not real!* I tried to tell myself that I was just tripping from sleep deprivation, but then again, if I did not point this stuff out, Sharon did, and we were seeing the same creatures doing the same things!

One night, when we went to get some more ice, Del, the dealer, asked me, "Have you seen the shadow people yet?"

I knew exactly what he was talking about. "What are they?"

"They're spirits," he replied, "but they won't hurt you."

Well, that was good to know, but then other things continued to happen. My girlfriend and I were doing our thing in bed, but instead of it being just the two of us, there seemed to be at least three women. The crazy thing was, I knew them by their voices but never saw their faces. After it was over, I would snap out of it and go about life.

I began feeling confused and guilty as if I was cheating on Sharon, so I sat her down and explained what was going on. I told her how bad I felt because I loved her so much. I asked if she could tell when I went there in my mind, and she said that I would get this look in my eyes.

We came up with a plan so that when it happened again, she was supposed to ask me who she was; so every now and then, she would say, "Who am I?"

When she would ask that, I was scared to death. I would say her name over and over in my head, knowing that if I said it, it was probably wrong; so a lot of times, I would say, "You're my girlfriend." That was good enough for her because she could see that I was struggling with it, so she would smile, and it was okay.

* * * * *

One morning, we couldn't get ahold of Del to get more meth, and Sharon began to make some of the scariest faces I have ever seen. I mean, it was horrifying. I asked her to please stop, but she didn't even know what I was talking about.

Later on, one night, I really badly wanted to take a shower. We went to my house where I had all the water I needed, so when we got there, I started to get out of the car. Then it started. Sharon wanted to tell me something. When she would finish telling me one thing, she would start on something else. She would always say, "Just a couple more minutes, please. I'm almost done."

As she rambled on, I told her, "I keep seeing your mom in the back seat." She actually turned around and looked, and then she laughed.

Things got quiet when both of us heard people talking, so we stopped and tried to listen. When we saw the people, they were walking dogs. It was almost 2:00 a.m. I did not recognize any voices, so we kept watching, and they seemed to go to my neighbor's house.

Then, they vanished.

While we were discussing what we saw, I could hear a couple of people running along the side of my house. I got out of the car with

Sharon right behind me. When we got to the corner of my house, there was nobody there. The streetlight was bright enough to where I could see, but not a soul was in sight.

We hurried into the house, and instantly, she started. On and on, she went. I seemed to be going in and out of it—seeing Sharon then another person. I went to sit down and finally made it to the couch as she carried on the whole way.

Then, she pointed and cried, "Look!"

I told her that I did not see anything. She began to explain that she had seen a groundhog and some other animal. It took a while for her to figure out that the other animal she saw was a hedgehog. She said that the groundhog was black with a white stripe going down its back.

"Are you sure that it wasn't a skunk?" I challenged. "Because a skunk is black with a white stripe."

"I know what a skunk is, and I know what a groundhog is," she replied, "and it was a groundhog." Then she began to tell me about the hedgehog and said it was purple.

When she told me that, boy, let me tell you, we both laughed so hard. Then almost in disbelief, she got up and showed me where they went behind the TV.

I wanted to get away from her, but Sharon caught up with me just as I made it to the bathroom door. She convinced me to go back and sit down on the couch, talking seductively. As I got settled, she would move to the couch, to the recliner, to the den table, then back to the couch. She would not stay long in one place. As she would move, she would change to a different female.

When I noticed a window of opportunity, I tried to get away again. I moved as fast as I could, but Sharon grabbed me by the shoulder, picked me up, and literally tossed me backward like a rag doll.

"Where do you think you're going? I am not done talking to you!"

"How did you do that?" I asked her, amazed at what she did.

It was incredible as little as she was. She could not really explain, just that the dope gave her super strength.

During this whole time, I could also see people walking around, both male and female. There were these two old men sitting at the table watching everything as it was going on. They never said a thing; they would just watch. I'd had enough. I was tired of them watching us, so I flipped them the middle finger. My girlfriend asked me what was going on, so I told her about the two old men watching us. Then she explained that there was not anyone there; it was just the drugs and me.

I went on and got my shower, but as I came out of the bathroom, I felt confused. *Where is everybody?* I was in disbelief. *No way,* I thought, *I saw other people. I know what I saw.* That was not good enough, so I went where the two old men had been sitting and just stared at the table, trying to imagine them sitting in the chairs. That didn't work, so I accepted it.

One morning, Sharon and I were sitting in my car. As we talked, I kept seeing people wandering outside and around the car. I even noticed my ex-wife who appeared to go inside my girlfriend's house. When I looked back, everyone else was gone. It was very puzzling. *Where did everyone go?* I just could not understand. *Why did everyone just up and leave?*

How Sharon did not notice me looking around while we were talking, I will never know. When I asked, "Where did everyone go?" she said, "Who?"

I began to explain about all the people I had seen outside. Just as she was explaining that there had been no one outside since we had been there, I snapped out of it.

* * * * *

One night, we went back to Sharon's place. When we walked in, there was this horrible disgusting smell—I mean, it was almost gagging me.

I asked her, "What is that smell?"

Of course, she had an answer. "It's the dope we've been smoking."

Well, what can I say? I asked, I got an answer, so I guess I had no choice but go with that answer?

Still running here and there, we were seeing the so-called shadow people—only at night, never in the light. They were almost in the same places every time. Sometimes, they would change things up here and there, and sometimes, a couple of them would act as if they were hiding, but they always made sure that we saw them.

I remember one standing at the side of the road. He seemed to be watching us as we drove by; we even slowed down. I will say this—this one rather gave me the willies. I thought to myself, *Why is he watching us?*

As I would see them in their groups, I would always wonder what they were talking about. They always seemed to be talking, but about what? Then again, they had no faces; they were just like a shadow made from the sun, so how could they be communicating? I couldn't help but wonder if it was real. It had to be because my girlfriend and I were seeing the very same thing.

I kept remembering what Del had said that one time. "*The shadow people are spirits, but they won't hurt you. They're harmless.*" So when Sharon and I would go out after dark, we would always look for them no matter where we would go. I began to notice that the more houses and people there were, the more shadow people there seemed to be. If I ever took Sharon to do her thing (usually shoplifting), I would often see the shadow people around. Watching them gave me something to do while I waited.

I still had lots of questions, though. Not just about the shadow people but other things like all the other women that would show up while I was in bed with my girlfriend. Del's girlfriend, Sarah, said that she had heard of other people experiencing the same thing, including her own boyfriend. Well, I got another answer, but I needed more. As time went on, I would ask questions and hunt them down, but the answers were just not good enough. I realized I had to personally seek out the answers.

So hold on and buckle your seat belt because the ride is getting ready to take off. It is going to get extremely crazy. Again I want to remind you that everything I am sharing is God's honest truth. He is the reason why I am still alive today and the reason that I can remember the details to tell you my story.

CHAPTER 3

The next thing I knew, Sharon found some old needles at her house. I didn't know that she had been shooting up during the time we had broken up. We had gone to get her a pill, and she was all over me about doing her leftovers. In other words, she wanted to know what was left in the spoon and filter that she did not get. I told her that I was forty-seven years old and not ever going to stick a needle in my arm.

As usual, she argued, "Give me your arm." We fussed over and over, "Give me your arm!" After about ten or fifteen minutes, I gave in. I really did not feel much—just a little tingly, a little light-headed, so what was so special about that?

As I began to travel down this road, I learned that the pavement does not last long. In fact, the road became very rough and curvy with lots of potholes. No 4×4 can travel on this road. To tell you the truth, I don't even think a tank can make it through. The only place it leads is straight to hell.

One thing usually leads to another, and in this case, it was heroin. Sharon wanted to try it, but I was completely against it. I made sure that she understood that I was in no way, shape, form, or fashion going to use heroin. See, I was very scared of it—people were dying from overdoses, aside from it being one of the most addictive drugs known to mankind.

We went to Del, and he fixed her up, explaining how to do it. I was right there the whole time, scared that if anything was to go wrong, she'd at least have me there. Immediately, she shot up half of what she had, and Del told her to save the rest for afterwhile. She started walking around murmuring, "I don't feel anything." Well, I thought differently because she had become very clumsy.

The next thing I knew, Del's girlfriend, Sarah, had made up a very potent shot and asked me if I wanted some of it. I told her I had no money and that Sharon had spent it all. "I didn't ask for money," she countered. "I asked if you wanted some of this."

Sarah squirted some in another shot and handed it to me. I had not graduated to shooting myself up yet, so I gave it to my girlfriend. When I did, she turned it upside down and poured it all out. Then she tilted the table over and spilled water all over their bed, all the while saying that she didn't feel anything. I finally got her to leave.

After being on the road for maybe five minutes, things took a curve, and what I witnessed was amazing. Sharon slipped down, lying in her car seat, twisting around as if she was making love. I tried to talk to her, but I don't think she could hear me. All she could say was, "What have you done to me? What are you doing?"

She continued wiggling in the seat, almost on the floor, pulling her shirt up, moaning, "I'm so hot, I'm burning up."

We were almost home, and things went back to normal. After we were there about fifteen minutes, Sharon wanted to do the rest of the heroin. After she did, there was a little left, and she really wanted me to have it. There was hardly anything, so I tried it. I did feel something, but not really anything to brag about.

After about ten minutes, she began to talk to at least three different girls. She was even calling them by their names. As I would talk to her, I don't even think she realized I was there. My girlfriend would just look at me and make horrible, nasty faces, never speaking to me. So I finally just sat back in the recliner, watched, and laughed.

After about twenty minutes, Sharon began to snap out of it. She asked me if she had been talking to someone, and I told her about the three girls. She said that she kind of remembered talking to them and who they were.

These were girls that Sharon and I knew, and as we were all becoming good friends, they had mentioned something about needing a place to stay until they saved up some money. They had been staying in motels for three or four days at a time, never more than a week. So Sharon left it up to me since it was my house. By this time, the house painting was completed, so everything was working out. Del and Sarah had moved in, and I told the girls that they could come and stay for a while. I gave them directions, and we came up with an agreement as to how we would work things out.

A couple of days later, they came over, and I gave them the choice of which bedroom they wanted. Things were going great—so I thought. Then one day, they went out, and my girlfriend and I waited for Del to come by with some ice. The girls came home later that night, and Del was very messed up. Sarah went into their room, and he came into the den where we were. He asked what we wanted. Of course, I said ice, and Sharon said heroin. As I was smoking the ice on aluminum foil, Del told Sharon that he would take care of her. I noticed how he was acting; he was in and out of it—mostly out of it. We had to keep saying his name in order to keep him coming back, even though he never really knew what was going on.

The next thing we knew, Del was dumping heroin all over the table. He was nodding out, almost falling over on the table. I was constantly talking to him. Then suddenly, he reared back to hit me. Right before he connected, and I mean inches from my face, he stopped.

"Oh, I'm sorry," he apologized. It was like nothing had ever happened.

Turning back to the heroin, he finally got their shot ready. While he was in the process of taking it, I told Sharon that I felt as if she was going to die from an overdose. "Everything's going to be okay," she assured me. "Del knows what he's doing."

He had just injected his shot of heroin, and she was still trying to hit the vein. The next thing I knew, he wouldn't respond to anything. "Something is wrong," I said. "He won't react to anything that I say."

Sharon began to yell out his name. "Del? Del!" Nothing. "Oh my god, his lips are blue." She got up out of the recliner and began pushing on him, hollering out his name. "*Del!*" He just kind of fell over and rolled into the floor. "Something's wrong!" she yelled at Sarah. "Get in here, hurry!"

Sarah had been a nurse at one time, but because of drugs, she was nothing but a dealer's girlfriend who had lost everything. When she came into the room, she realized he was not breathing. She felt for a pulse, but there was nothing. He was burning up, so she grabbed a glass of water to try to cool his body temperature. One thing about heroin that I learned was that it raises your body temperatures to dangerously high levels.

Sarah announced, "Someone is going to have to do chest compressions."

My girlfriend, who was crying and freaking out, got down and began chest compressions while Sarah was breathing for him. After a few minutes, she determined, "Someone is going to have to call 911."

I finally took over, not knowing what I was doing. As I worked on Del, Sarah explained to me how many times I needed to do chest compressions before she would breathe for him. Let me tell you, I hope I never have to do that again in my life. The sounds that he would make were horrifying, and the way his legs would draw up was an experience that no one should ever have to go through.

Before dialing the emergency number, Sarah had Sharon try to get ahold of our friend, Little Man, who had brought him back before. When Little Man answered the phone, he said that he had run out of gas and was needing help himself. Come to find out, this was the third time Del had died from an overdose. Not only that, but he had told his girlfriend that he was going to kill himself by overdosing. She had blown it off and didn't take him seriously.

Sharon ended up calling 911 and said that a friend of ours had stopped breathing and had no pulse. During this time, Del kind of came to but went back out. Sarah kept calling out, "You're not dying! Please don't leave me like this, I love you. Please!"

Then, it was like a miracle—he sprung up on his feet in a kind of speed mode like he was fixing to run a race, continuously changing directions. He was sweating and very confused, asking, "What happened?" Sarah explained that he had died and that we had brought him back. He was in disbelief, scoffing, "No, I didn't!"

This would go on for a couple of minutes until she got him to sit down on the couch, waiting on the paramedics. He did not want to hang around because he knew the police would be coming too.

Suddenly, reality hit, and Sarah cried out, "Get rid of everything, the police will be here!" Come to find out that Del had been doing speedballs before this. A speedball is a mixture of an upper and a downer. In his case, it was a mixture of ice (upper) and heroin (downer). Speedballs are very popular and very deadly. Many ordinary people, as well as movie stars, have lost their lives because of them. Not all speedballs are made exactly the same; just as long as there is an upper and a downer together in a person's system, it is considered a speedball.

After a moment, Sarah asked, "What did you do with everything?" We told her that we had taken everything to my room and hid it. "You don't understand," she pleaded, "the police will search the house! Get it out of here—get it out of the house before they get here!"

We were in a panic trying to get rid of it all. Finally, everything was hidden outside, and we went back to see how the dealer was doing. Sarah was keeping him as calm as possible. He was soaking wet, not able to sit still, freaking out because he knew the police were on their way. Again she asked us, "Are you sure that you all got everything out of the house? Because they will search it."

I don't know why, but it seemed to take a little while for the police and paramedics to make their way to my house. Then again, that was good because it gave us plenty of time to calm down. Once we started hearing sirens, we knew it was getting close to the time of reckoning. I went out in the front yard and met the police as they pulled up. I don't remember what I said; it really didn't matter because they had one thing on their minds and one thing only.

"Where is he?" the officer asked. As we were approaching the door to the house, reality smacked me in the face, and I began to realize how serious this really was. Another police car arrived, then the fire truck, and then the ambulance. It was starting to get crazy.

CHAPTER 4

As I walked into the house, the police were at work questioning Del the dealer. They wanted to know what he had been doing and what he was on. "We're not stupid," they told him. "You're soaking wet, you can't sit still, and you look horrible." So again they asked, "What kind of drugs have you been doing?"

At this point, the paramedics stepped in and said that they needed to talk with him and make sure he was okay. So they began with the questions, asking what kind of drugs he'd been doing. Still, Del was giving the same answer, "Haven't been doing any drugs."

As the paramedics worked with him, the policemen began questioning us. They asked who we all were and took Sharon's ID because she'd made the call, and he was not dead.

Sarah, Del's girlfriend, told the officer that he was homeless. She said that they were friends and that he had called to tell her that he didn't have anywhere to stay, so she'd picked him up, and they'd called us. She also told them that when she'd picked him up, he had acted normal, and everything seemed okay. She explained that the two of them had not really known us long, but she'd called us because she knew we were nice people.

Meanwhile, the paramedics were still trying to get an answer out of Del. One of the police officers decided it was time to step in. He began with the threats. "If you don't tell us what you have been doing, there are ways around this." He continued, "You can either tell them, or we can take you ourselves and get a blood sample because it's obvious that you've been doing something, and we want to know what it is."

I could not believe how all this was coming together; it was as if we had rehearsed it. His girlfriend and I were standing in the kitchen watching all this go on, and Sharon was still sitting in the recliner. Then the officer that took Sharon's ID asked her to step outside. You could tell by the look in her eyes that she was worried. As the screen door was closing, I heard the handcuffs. To make a long story short, she had a warrant out of Florida for failure to appear.

After that happened, I noticed the policemen kind of wandering around the house with their flashlights on. Then I noticed a flashlight at the bottom of the couch. That kind of hit a spot inside me. I thought, *I did not look under the couch to make sure that nothing had been dropped.* I mean, my eyes were following the light the entire time. After a while, the lights were turned off.

Then, it happened—the mistake that almost caused me to have a heart attack. The flashlight came back on and went straight to the end table. On it was a piece of aluminum foil that I had been smoking on. The only thing going for me was that it was folded up, but still, it was noticed. The flashlight was turned back off, and suddenly, the attention was back on Del. I thought, *Thank God!* because I believed that since it was my house, I'd be in a lot of trouble.

But it wasn't over. The flashlight came back on and again went to the piece of aluminum foil on the table. The policeman was very curious. My heart began to race because then he took the pen that he had in his pocket and began to unfold the foil. *It's over,* I thought. *Busted! It's my turn—I am going to jail.* Then a miracle—the officer turned his light off and lost interest.

By this time, Del had admitted to using (I just do not remember *what* he said he had been using). So they loaded him up in the ambulance, and everyone left. Sarah and I talked about what had happened. The one thing that kept coming up was the flashlight and the aluminum foil. She said that she had also been freaking out over it.

I kept trying to call Sharon's mom Sheila to tell her what had happened. I never was able to get ahold of her, so I just decided that I would go to her house and tell her. In the meantime, Sarah had been talking to Little Man. He was less than a mile up the road. That worked out great because it was on the way to Sheila's house.

When we got ready to leave, there were still a couple of police cars sitting in front of the house. They were just shooting the bull, maybe even doing paperwork—who knows? I did notice that Sharon was still in the back of one of the cruisers. Of course, they would not let me tell her goodbye. So as we were leaving, I made sure that I drove by her so I could see her one more time before they took her away.

When we picked up Little Man, Sarah wanted me to take her back to the house. Come to find out that she knew Sharon's mom, and they did not get along. (Apparently, the two of them had once gotten into it at a wedding.) Still, I made them ride with me to Sheila's. When we got there, she was amazed, not because her daughter was going to jail but because of how it happened.

After that, we went on back to the house. I began smoking ice—it was like nothing had ever happened. I went into my room, and Sarah started going through my girlfriend's stuff. She asked me if this was Sharon's stuff she was selling. I let her have some of it, mostly the things that still had tags on them. To me, that meant more ice.

A couple of hours passed, and Sarah reminded me that she and Little Man needed to go to the hospital and check on Del. After a couple of more hours, she said it again. They finally left.

They came back after two or three hours, and Del was with them. He really did not look good and still seemed puzzled, almost scared. As he walked by, I asked him how he was, and he really did not want to talk. Later on, that night, Del came up to me, and what he said to me I will never forget. "Why did you not let me die? I told them that I was going to kill myself."

I was amazed, shocked, and in disbelief at what had come out of his mouth. "Are you kidding me? You're not dying in my house!"

Then, Del remarked, "By the way, you didn't do nothing for me. My girlfriend kept me alive by breathing for me—not you."

"You tell me that all the chest compressions I did were for nothing?" I countered. "I get no credit?"

"What you did was nothing," he said. "It was my girlfriend, all her. She kept me alive, not you."

Let me tell you, you think someone has told you something that made you feel like nothing; this made me feel empty. I was in shock. I could not believe what I had heard.

One night, not long after that, Little Man was gone, and Sarah was sleeping. Del asked me if I wanted to make some runs for him. The first one he needed me for was about ten minutes away. As I was driving down the road, I began to think about everything he had said. It was really bothering me. I finally decided that I needed to say something—I needed to get it off my chest. So after I made the run, I confronted Del about what he had said and how I thought it wasn't fair that I didn't get any credit at all for helping to keep him alive. Then it came out. "I'm sorry for saying what I did," he apologized. "I don't know why I said that."

I asked Del if he would fix me up a small shot of heroin. He got it together and explained how I would go about sticking the needle in my vein, pulling up blood, and then injecting. Well, when I picked it up, I just could not seem to figure it out. It felt weird. I just couldn't do it.

I finally got Del to give it to me. I didn't feel anything, so I asked him to do it again. "After you get back from this last run," he bargained.

When I got back from the run (which was the same place again), he fixed me up. "Look, do you see what's in it?" he asked. When I looked in the spoon, not only was there heroin but also a little piece of ice. Imagine that—a speedball! When the piece of ice dissolved, Del pulled it up in the rig (the shot). He hit me with the needle, and in a few minutes, I began feeling very sick.

The next thing I knew, I was sweating so bad that within seconds, I was soaking wet. By the time Del came to check on me, I had moved from the recliner to the floor. He told me that I needed to take a shower and go to bed. "There is no way that I can take a shower!" I argued. "I am too sick and sweating too bad."

Del went back to his room, and as he was going in, I thought, *Why is he going into Sharon's room?* So I made myself get up to see what was going on. When I got to his room, I realized that she was still in jail. I told him what I thought had happened. I don't remember what was said; I just remember leaving his bedroom, making it back to the chair, and lying across the back of it because I felt so sick.

After a few minutes, I gathered my clothes, got a towel, and went to take my shower. Afterward, I went straight to bed. When I lay down and my head hit the pillow, that was it. I was gone, literally out like a light.

CHAPTER 5

As time would go on with this addiction, I would have my friends hit me every now and then with the needle, but mostly, I was still smoking it—ice, meth—whatever you want to call the junk that it is.

I began to feel something crawling on me, little tickling sensations all over. I asked Del and Sarah if they knew anything about it. They explained that it was the dope coming out of my skin. I began to look for it as I felt it. I noticed that when my body warmed up, it would start coming out. Then I started to *see* it—it looked like a little bubble coming out of my skin. *This is crazy!* I thought. *I can actually see the dope coming out.*

One day, I was at my friend's house, and it was getting warm. I started to notice that crawling feeling, like the stuff was coming out of my skin. I got in the shade, found sunlight coming through a small spot, and watched it. Then I thought of something. I hollered at my friend's mom and told her I wanted to show her something. My friend's mom does not do drugs, and she doesn't drink. She is a very honest woman who is a Christian and takes care of her mom. So I said, "Look."

As I held my arm up at the little beam of light coming through the leaves, she admitted, "I don't see anything."

So I put my finger next to it and directed, "Look by my finger, look real close."

"What is that?" she wondered. I could not believe that she might be seeing something. I asked if she really saw anything. "I saw

34

something," she confirmed. "What is it?" I told her that it was the dope coming out of my skin.

Eventually, the crawling sensation led to other things. I started scratching. It wasn't bad, but what that would lead to would be called picking. Picking is when a person picks at their skin until there is a scab. Some people that get desperate for dope will actually eat their scabs in order to keep going. Not only that, they will even drink their pee because there's so much dope in it. I became a picker, but I can honestly say I never ate my scabs or drank my pee. To me, that was disgusting.

One afternoon, I went to my mom and dad's house to visit. While I was there, they asked me to have supper with them. I didn't have many scabs on me, but my dad noticed the places on my arm. He asked me if I was doing meth because he had heard about the sores that some people would get because of the drug. I had no shame and answered him truthfully. He told me that if I needed or wanted help with this addiction, then he would get me help.

Like I said, I had no shame in this game of addiction. I was raising my three children five days a week. It took me six days on this junk to lose them. I admit, yes, it was my fault and only my fault. I have no one to blame but myself. My phone was messing up, and I didn't call them because I didn't want to lie and tell them I was coming home when I knew I wasn't. So I lost them due to abandonment. Let me ask you a question: Do you think that phased me one bit? The answer is *no*! And to beat it all, it had barely gotten started.

The picking was getting worse. I was actually taking a fishhook and breaking the skin to start the whole process. People would tell me to stop. I would tell them I couldn't. Depending on where I was and who was around, I would hide it. I even got to where I would pull the legs of my shorts up when I picked them so people couldn't see the new places that I was making.

I started noticing something different about the house. I really could not explain what it was—just something different. It was as if the house itself was changing. Then this horrible, disgusting smell would just appear. It was like burning chemicals.

This made me ask questions. I needed answers for everything that was going on. So I asked Del and his girlfriend, "Do you all smell that horrible, disgusting smell?"

They both gave the same answer, "It's the dope coming out of our skin."

I came back with, "If that's the dope coming out of our skin, then would we not smell it all the time, as much dope as we do?"

They replied, "You just don't notice it all the time."

I asked them about the house and how it seemed to be changing. Their answer was that when the dope was gone out of the house, things would go back to normal. That was something I just could not understand—when the dope was gone, the house would go back to normal? At that time, I had no choice but to accept the answer that I had. Later on, I was determined to find out the truth, and it's something I'll share when it's time—the problem is, can you handle the truth?

CHAPTER 6

One night, I was sitting on the couch when I found something unusual. I don't remember where Del and Sarah were—probably gone somewhere. A lot of times, they would leave at night and not come back, sometimes till morning.

The thing that I found was like a creature, perfectly round. It was made out of what seemed to be a bunch of cocoons. Not only that, it was really hairy, and as I examined it, the hairs seemed to be moving like it was alive.

It freaked me out. It reminded me of a spider, and spiders and I do not get along. I dropped the thing on the floor, went to get something to pick it up, and threw it away in the trash can.

When Del and Sarah got home, I told them about what I had found and described it to them. I went back to the trash can, looked around, and could not find it—but of course, they had an answer. They told me that it was my imagination and that it was not real; it was just a lack of sleep. Well, the answer was not good enough for me. I knew what I had seen. I had it in my hands and had even examined it.

Things were getting bad between them. They would bust out in some of the craziest fights, which would last fifteen to twenty minutes. I would try to intervene, but Little Man would stop me. "Leave them alone, let them get it out. I'll make sure he doesn't hurt her." The funny thing was that while the fighting was going on, he would look back at me and smile like he was really having fun.

The fighting was getting worse. I mean every day, maybe even two or three times a day, over things that made no sense, no reason, just plain stupid. Then one morning, Sarah screamed for help. When I got to their bedroom, Del had her pinned down on the bed and had his fist pulled back, fixing to hit her. It was like he was being fully controlled by something. I hollered at him to stop. Del looked at me as if he was surprised but confused. Then he straightened up and just walked away like nothing ever happened.

* * * * *

A few days later, I was walking through the house when I heard someone coming up behind me. I turned around to see who it was – but nobody was there. *Okay,* I thought, *I swear that I heard footsteps.*

I went on my way and again heard someone walking up behind me. This time, I was sure. Waiting until they got right behind me, I jumped up and spun around to catch them off guard, hoping to scare them.

Again, no one, *but I* know *I heard someone!*

Later on, I heard footsteps again. This time, I really paid attention, making sure that it truly was someone behind me. Right when they got behind me, I jumped up and spun around again—still, *nobody.* I was beginning to think that I was crazy, but I knew it had happened. I cannot tell you how many times that happened that day, but it happened a lot.

The next time I heard footsteps, I turned around, and there was Del. When I saw him, it scared the crap out of me. I was not expecting someone behind me like so many times before. I never said a word to anyone because after hearing him come up on me from behind, I know that what I heard was real. I just could not come up with an answer.

* * * * *

As the night would come about, I loved it. I just could not get enough of the dark. The one thing that I could always count on was being able to watch the shadow people and try to figure out what they were doing. They would usually be in the same spot, but every now and then, they would throw a curveball. In the end, they would let you know that it was them.

One time, I was walking down the hall toward my bedroom. Just as I passed the bathroom, something told me to look in there. As I walked in, something told me to look in the trash can. There were a couple of pieces of paper in it, hardly anything. So I picked the paper up, and I could not believe my eyes. The round cocoon-like thing that I had found by the couch that one night was right there in the trash can, exactly where the voice told me to look. I mean, it was identical except that it had a piece of plastic coming out of it, the width of the cocoons.

It was upright, and I was amazed that the hairs coming out of it were doing something like a wave. It was alive, almost like it was trying to get me to pick it up. I decided that when Del and Sarah left, I would get that round thing and take it to my room where I could examine it closer.

I was careful and covered it back up, not wanting anyone to see it because if it was real, it was mine. Everything was going as planned, and they got ready to leave. As soon as they pulled out, I ran to the bathroom to get my discovery. When I got there, I could not believe my eyes—the trash can was empty. Someone had emptied the trash, even though there hadn't been that much, just a couple of pieces of paper. So I went to the trash can in the kitchen pantry to look for it. Nothing—it was gone. Why?

* * * * *

Eventually, I let Little Man move in. Del and Sarah were still fighting all the time, and Del left for a little while. When he came back, he brought a couple of girls I had never met. Del introduced me to them and left with one of them. The one who stayed behind was named Kristi. She was beautiful, not that the other girl wasn't pretty, but Kristi was so beautiful and very young. She was there for Little Man, to be his companion until whenever.

We talked for a while when Kristi told me that she had OD'd twice. She almost seemed to be proud of it. Then she gave me a bag of ice and told me that she had some more for after a while. I went to my room and was not there long when Little Man hollered for me to come. I hurried in there and saw that Kristi had spilled her ice, pills, and heroin on the floor. Little Man asked if I could find her stuff because I could find anything in the carpet if I knew the general area. I had become a pro at this because I would often spend hours looking for dope that may have been dropped by me or anyone else.

I set to work, and they went back to his room. It took me seconds to find the heroin and pills, but the ice, I never found. Actually, if the heroin hadn't been in the form that it was in, I would have never found it. This heroin looked like a little wood chip, while all the others were in fine powder form, almost like dust. Kristi was amazed at how fast I found everything. To tell you the truth, I was amazed myself. Then again, the saying is: "Practice makes perfect," and all the time that I spent digging in the carpet was getting my practice in for times like that one.

Kristi gave me a bag of ice for my "good deeds," so of course, I didn't waste much time and got high. I noticed that the door to Little Man's room was open, and something told me that I should check on them. When I looked in there, Little Man and Kristi were on the floor—he was lying down with his head in her lap while she was rubbing and patting his head. They seemed like they were in a different world.

When I saw this, it took me back to a story that I had heard. It was said that when people would do this, one of them would die, and the other one wouldn't know because of the state of mind that they were in. Then by the time it was discovered that one was dead, it would be too late because too much time had passed, and there would be no chance of bringing them back.

So thinking back to that story, I would check on them every now and then. I would even go in there and stand over them to make sure they were breathing. The whole time I was freaking out—I mean, I was scared to death! I did not want to go through almost losing someone again. Still to this day, as I write this, it amazes me how a person can be so far out of it that they don't even know that death is knocking at their door—or even know that life exists.

In between this time and coming back to reality, Kristi and Little Man would run back and forth to the shower. This was incredible because they would act as if they were little kids playing. I mean, really, if you did not know their ages and happened to come into my house and heard them, you would have wondered what was going on.

After a couple of days, they kind of came around—back to life, back to reality. Kristi asked me if she could move in, and I said that she could. She gave me her phone number, and then they left to go try to make some money because they were out of dope. They knew that if they didn't get anything soon, they would be getting dope sickness.

To get dope sickness is horrifying, depending upon what kind of dope and how much a person is used to using. It's a nightmare that can last a couple of weeks. Sometimes, death seems to be the only way out because of the mental anguish, sickness, and body aches that come as a result of the addiction.

A couple of hours passed, Little Man came back, but Kristi was not around. I asked where she was, and he told me that they had run into one of her ex-boyfriends. She had gone with him. I called her the next day, and we talked for a little while (maybe one more time after that), but beyond that, she wouldn't answer the phone. Still to this day, I do not know what happened to Kristi; I just hope that she is alive because as long as she is alive, there is hope.

CHAPTER 7

Before long, I picked up a new habit. Where it came from, I have no idea, but I began to get creative with aluminum foil. I would spend not only hours but days, weeks, and even a couple of months playing with it and shaping it to make things.

The first things were boxes, boxes of all kinds, shapes, and sizes—ring boxes, knife boxes, and boxes to put gifts in. The boxes even had lids to go with them. When I would make a box or anything else, I would add enough aluminum foil to make it sturdy. There were even a couple of people who thought my work was pretty neat and even asked if they could have some of my creations.

I began to get even more creative and learned to make bowls and cups. I carried on for weeks until I came up with a brilliant idea: I would make a cross that would be two pieces so there would be room to put stuff inside of it. As I focused on making it, Del and a couple of other people would ask me if I was okay—they thought I had lost my mind.

I was still talking to Sharon on the phone about every day, but by this time, she had been transported to a prison in Florida. The crazy thing was that every time she called, I seemed to be playing with aluminum foil.

Time went on, and I started to notice things happening at night that could not be explained. I decided to investigate, so the first thing I went for was my flashlight. In the ice (meth) world, flashlights are a must; actually, the more flashlights, the better. One night, I was by myself when I got my little flashlight out of my pocket along with my knife. They usually always stayed in my pocket because if something of this sort was not nailed down, it would somehow disappear. All I needed was a spoon, and I had stashed spoons everywhere, so if I ever needed one in an emergency, *bingo*! I had one.

I proceeded to one of the bedrooms, and as I was headed that way, my girlfriend came up behind me and purred, "What are you doing?"

I could see her beautiful blond hair behind me, and her voice was very different. I loved to hear her speak; I thought it was sexy. I got so nervous; I was almost scared to answer, but then again, what was I going to say?

See, I was scared because Sharon had already told me that she thought I was going crazy, so I just came out and told her what I was doing—that I was going to look around with my flashlight to see what I could find and look for change.

She spoke, "Get glitter."

"Glitter?" I repeated.

"Yes, from the glitter bugs."

"The glitter bugs?"

"Yes," Sharon directed and stretched her arm out. "Here." We walked into the bedroom. "See?"

I turned my flashlight on and shined it on the bed. To my amazement, there was glitter on it—not much, but there was some glitter. I held my flashlight in my mouth, spoon in one hand, knife in the other, and went to town collecting glitter.

As it seemed that I had gathered almost all the glitter, something told me to pat the bed because the bed was kind of fuzzy. When I would pat the bed, glitter would just appear. I would begin again, mashing the spoon down into the bed and knocking the glitter into it with the knife. As I continued on, I would take the glitter that I had collected in the spoon and put it on the desk behind me because I did not want to spill it.

Even as I worked on collecting the glitter, I would be seeing the glitter bugs. I watched them to see if I could catch one. Every now and then, I would see an opportunity. I would move as quickly as possible before the glitter bug went back down into the comforter, trying to catch it with the spoon and knife. Let me tell you that I tried at least four times, but they escaped capture every time. A couple of times, I came close that it seemed as if I had one in the spoon; but for some reason, I just could not keep one of the glitter bugs there.

It had started breaking daylight; I could see that the light was beginning to come through the window, and it seemed as if I got all the glitter because I couldn't find any more. I was proud of myself and could not wait to show my girlfriend all the glitter I had collected for her.

Just as I went into the den, I began to wonder what was going on because I realized that Sharon was not actually there—she was in jail. I thought, *I am not crazy, this was not a hallucination!* I talked to her. I heard her voice, and I saw her beautiful, long blond hair behind me. Why did I not turn around? Then I thought, *I would have never known about the glitter and glitter bugs if she had not shown me.*

I kept thinking that I needed an answer really bad because this was not right! What was going on? I knew that the answers I had found did not point to me as being insane. Then it occurred to me, *If I am insane, then there won't be a pile of glitter on the desk where I put it.*

I went back to the room and looked on the desk where I had collected the glitter. I was amazed at what I was seeing—there was a pile of glitter about as big around as a dime and about as tall as maybe two dimes. Also, to my amazement, the glitter was in a neat pile. I just could not understand all of this. I kept going over and over it in my head, trying to come up with an explanation for what was going on because it was real.

Not long after that, Del came home, and I began to explain everything to him. I showed him the glitter, and he kind of acted like he cared, but I could tell he really didn't. Then Little Man came home, and I told him everything. He seemed to be a little more interested, but before it was over, he just blew it off and said I was tripping.

I decided to get the glitter, put it in something, and save it. When I got back to the room, to my amazement, the glitter was gone. I confronted both of them, and they swore that they had done nothing with it. There was no explaining how it just—*poof*—disappeared!

* * * * *

I continued working with aluminum foil, making all kinds of things, but mainly working on the cross. I wanted to give it to Sharon, and I began to really get creative with it. I started adding some pieces to the sides to make it more even as the cross had begun to take a form to where the outer rim was a little higher.

Then, something crazy happened; for some reason, I turned to talk to Sharon who was on the couch behind me while I was at the kitchen table working on the foil cross. When I turned to look at her, I was puzzled beyond puzzled. She was gone. *Where is she? She was just here.* Then I reasoned, *But she can't be here. She's in jail!* Then I began to cry like a baby, I mean, seriously, bawling like a baby. My head dropped onto the arm that was on the table, and I began to laugh at myself, and when I say *laugh*, I mean literally laugh. *This is crazy!* I told myself. *Why would I do this, knowing that I know she's in jail in Florida?*

I don't know why, but I thought Sharon was behind me again, so I turned to look at her. *I just went through this!* I reminded myself, so the process started all over. I started bawling like a baby then realized again that I was being crazy and started laughing at myself like an insane person. Then again, ditto—again—over and over and over. I cannot tell you how long I did this, but it happened many times.

I do remember this: the more it happened, it got to where I was not crying or laughing. I was just turning around to see her. I was getting faster and faster. Then I kind of came to my senses, got up, and walked through the den. As I went by the couch, where I thought she had been sitting, I looked again. I pleaded with myself, *Why, why do I keep turning to see her?* Then it hit me, *something* kept telling me that Sharon was behind me because come to think of it, there was something on the couch acting like her. *I am not crazy!* I thought to myself. There had to have been something there because I wouldn't have done what I did if there hadn't been. As usual, I had no answer to this. *No way,* I thought. *There is no way that I am tripping because this was real.*

* * * * *

45

One night, Little Man had an idea. "Let's go out in the garage and look around." So we went out there, and he began going through stuff. While he was busy, I went to the side door of the garage and looked outside. There in the backyard, I saw something that I had never seen before. I glanced back at Little Man, and he was still just going through everything. Peering outside again, I could tell that what I was seeing was still there. I shook my head to clear it like maybe I was trying to make what I was seeing disappear. Then I looked again. It was still there.

What I saw appeared to be an old woman with long hair wearing a robe. She was almost white with a gray tint to her. The robe and her hair were moving softly as if there was a small breeze. I tried to figure out what could be making me see this. I asked Little Man to look outside and tell me what he saw out there. (I didn't tell him what I had seen.) He looked and immediately turned around and started looking in the garage.

I noticed that he was not the same and seemed to be agitated. "Did you see it?"

"Yes!"

"Did you see the old woman that was white, wearing the gown?"

He answered, "No, what I saw was black and scary!"

Then, I went back and looked again. The old woman that I had seen was still there! To this day, I think of what I saw that night and what Little Man saw, and I can say that it was good, not bad—maybe even a guardian angel!

CHAPTER 8

Before I continue, I want to remind you that all of this is true. I feel like I have to say this because many people might think that I'm crazy that it was just the drug. I myself find it hard to believe, but I lived this nightmare.

A few weeks passed, and it was getting really close for my girlfriend to get out of jail. I had been keeping in contact with her mom Sheila, sharing information. We had also decided that I would go with Sharon's parents to pick her up when she got out. I was told not to worry about anything on this trip and that everything would be taken care of.

Sharon had almost convinced me that the pill addiction was under control. You see, the meth/ice addiction seemed okay because she was so easy to get along with, but on a pill, I used to tell people that horns came out of her head. There were a few people who understood and did not want her around when she was on a pill. Sharon's mom would even ask why she was so mean to me. She'd put up with it for a little while but would tell Sharon to leave because she was not going to listen to her mouth and put up with her.

Then again, her mom would feed her pill addiction. Sheila would keep track of all the money, and when Sharon would get out of jail, Sheila would eventually start giving her pills again, telling her, "I can't keep giving you pills without you paying for them because you owe me so much already."

So Sharon would start stealing in order to pay back her mom for everything, even the pills Sheila gave her. At the same time, this usually always kept Sharon in debt so that Sheila had control. She would always be making money off of her own daughter, and I mean an abundance of money. This girlfriend of mine, I used to feel so sorry for her; I actually still do. How can a person feel loved, especially when their own mom uses and abuses them through this kind of action? Still, I had been talking to Sheila while Sharon was in jail, and she swore that her daughter would never get another pill from her again.

It was the night before we had to leave. It was getting late, and I needed to finish the cross I had been making out of aluminum foil for Sharon. The design had shaped into where it looked like another cross kind of rose up off of it in three pieces. The three pieces were inset because of the way that the sides ended up. I was amazed at how awesome it looked. I wondered how I was able to make something so detailed out of aluminum foil. Seriously, it was so cool, and I was proud of what I had done. The dealer's friend came in, and I showed him what it had developed into. I couldn't believe what I heard come out of his mouth because he was one of the people who thought I had a problem with aluminum foil. "I can't believe what you have done! It actually looks pretty cool."

So he left, and I began to panic because I didn't have much time to finish. I still don't know why I did this, but I got a pair of scissors and began to cut on the cross, thinking that something needed to be fixed. I cut more and more. I couldn't stop because the more I cut, the more I needed to cut; it was driving me crazy. Then something came over me. It's kind of hard to explain, but I felt enraged. I lost it and took the cross and slung it across the room.

I watched as it hit the ceiling and crashed to the floor. I could not believe what I had just done. I got up, went to the mangled cross, and could not believe my eyes. How could I have done this? All the work that I had put into it was over in a flash. To look at it, you would have had no idea what you were looking at. You would have thought it was just a pile of aluminum foil. Then again, when I looked at it, it was a joke, a twisted pile of *Why did I do this?*

The time finally came to leave. "Yea!" I'd been hanging around with another dealer, sort of a young guy named Jeremy. His girlfriend, Karen, had told me that she thought I had been making things up this whole time about having a girlfriend; but here I was, setting off for Florida.

Sheila and I had already arranged to caravan together to Florida. The plan was that I would drive separately so that Sharon and I would have a car for us. As I was following Sharon's parents on the interstate, though, I could not stay awake. We were only an hour into the trip, and I had almost run into the back of their vehicle a couple of times. They got off at the next exit and asked me what the problem was. I told them that I couldn't stay awake, so her mom drove one vehicle, and her dad drove my car. We ended up having to go back home to leave my car, and then we all rode together in their vehicle.

We finally got to Florida—trust me, they know Florida like the back of their hand. They used to go to the beach every month because of the money they could make off their daughter stealing for them in order to get another pill. (As I write this book, my now-ex-girlfriend is back in jail in Florida. It's sad, but no surprise there.)

While we were waiting, Sheila announced, "I'm tired of waiting on her. It's about time to go to the motel. She can call us when she's ready."

"If you all leave, you can leave me here," I told them. "I'll wait on Sharon because I want to be here the minute she gets out." Thank God they didn't leave because I had no idea what was going on, no idea where I was, and no idea what to expect.

When Sharon came out, I was so excited that I wanted to cry. I got out of the vehicle and met her with a hug, telling her that I loved her. I am sure that she told me that too, but it wasn't long before she started in on me. She began to put me down because of the scars that were on me from picking.

We'd barely gotten down the road when Sharon pulled out some money and began to count it. She looked at me and said, "Yes, I have this leftover from jail. It's what you sent to me, and I'm not giving it back because you owe it to me."

Then, she counted out a certain amount and said, "Here, Mom. Do you have one of those for me?"

Remember that Sheila had sworn that her daughter would never, ever get another pill from her again, yet she did not hesitate and handed over her favorite pill: Opana, an opioid painkiller. We didn't even get ten to fifteen minutes down the road, and the pill was already crushed and up my girlfriend's nose.

As I watched this, I could not believe it. I even had tears drop out of my eyes. Sharon looked at me and asked what my problem was. I told her I couldn't believe my eyes. To make a long story short, I got my butt chewed out. I think it was around 4:30 a.m. before I got to bed. When I woke back up, Sharon was still on fire, being mean.

"Have you already had a pill?" I asked her. She proceeded to say that it made no difference and was none of my business.

I begged her mother, "Please ask her to stop! I need you to help me." Well, Sheila said that she could not help me, and if we couldn't get along, then I needed to get a bus ticket.

I decided to hang around.

Later that day, we all ended up going shopping. Not really because Sharon's mom and dad would go into a store ahead of her and pick out stuff that they wanted. She would watch them to see where they would lay things down then go to work. If an item had safety tags, no problem, she could remove those at no extra charge. The harder something was to get, the more she liked it. I guess it was the rush of getting away with it. Another way to say it might be "chasing the buzz from the pill to feed the addiction."

The term *chasing* to me means trying to feed the high so you don't lose it. You must chase whatever it takes to keep you high. I am against stealing, but I felt like I had no choice. In order to be with Sharon, I had to go. Most of the time, I stayed outside waiting and hoping to see my beautiful true love. "Love is blind," is that not what they say?

I did go into the store a couple of times, and let me tell you, I do not have the nerves that it takes to do this. I refused to help her, but at the same time, she would explain everything: who to watch, and I mean literally, she would explain their body movements to where they were looking and the location certain people were. Don't forget you have to keep video cameras in mind. I mean, this was like science. If all classes in school were as hard and complicated as this, I would have failed every class. Seriously, to do all this, you would have to have eyes in the back of your head—and I know for a fact that she did not, so I guess that's why she kept going to jail for the same thing.

After all this went down, we finally had enough of each other. Thank God for the family that He gave me because if it had not been for them, I have no idea how things would have played out. I called my niece, and she set me up a taxi to the bus station and a ticket to get me home.

I got to the bus station early. I was kind of confused because I had never been on a bus. The trip was supposed to take twelve to fourteen hours. I had no money, no food, and nothing to drink. I began freaking out about what I was going to do. My parents were on their way to the lake, so I called my sister, and she sent me twenty dollars for snacks and drinks. By the time I got home, I had two pennies left in my pocket.

Little Man and Jeremy had become really good friends to me, so on the way home, I actually told them where my car was so they could use it and come get me from the bus station. We got maybe thirty to forty minutes out, and I started calling but, of course, no answer. By the time I got to the bus station, I called my trustworthy dad who has always been there for me. I certainly don't mean to leave my mom out because I am a momma's boy and proud of it! Still to this day, at forty-eight years old, I feel the same way and believe that I was blessed with the family that I was born into.

CHAPTER 9

Home sweet home; there is nothing like home! When I got back, Dad dropped me off at my driveway, and my car was there. I went inside to find Little Man passed out in my recliner. Well, he had no idea what world he was in because he had done no telling how much heroin.

As I was trying to talk to him, someone whistled in one of the back bedrooms. I mean, it was loud. Now remember that I had just gotten home and had not had any dope for a couple of days. Besides that, Del and Sarah had moved out a few weeks before that, so I didn't think anyone else was home. I ran to the back of the house to see who had whistled, but nobody was there. This happened a couple of more times and still—*nobody*. Well, I finally just blew it off when I would hear that whistle.

It got to the point where I was using it as often as possible. Actually, I had become a pro at hitting my vein. People started asking me about Sharon; after all, she was the whole reason I had gone to Florida. "Stick a fork in me, I am done," I would tell everyone. "I cannot put up with the abuse anymore." As far as I was concerned, we were through.

After about a week, the phone rang, but I didn't recognize the number. I always answer the phone whether or not I know who it is, just because you never know. Lo and behold, it was Sharon. She was about two hours out and wanted to know if I could get any ice. I made a call, but they had run out. It just so happened that I had enough to take care of her—not much, just enough to make a shot for her. So when she got to her mom's, I wasted no time and went to pick her up. Apparently, we were on again. Things were going pretty well; I was amazed at how well we were getting along. Then again, she was not using pills at the time.

It wasn't long, though, before we were fighting again, usually over something stupid. One night, it got bad enough to where she picked up a coffee cup off the counter and warned, "If you do not get out of my face, I will hit you."

Well, stupid me took a step forward and said, "No!"

Big mistake.

The next thing I heard was the sound of that coffee cup as she whacked me in the head with it. To make matters worse, it was my favorite cup and the biggest one at that. So next thing I knew, I was picking myself up off the floor. The handle was still in Sharon's hand, and the cup was on the floor. I was in shock, absolutely baffled that she had whacked me upside the head. "I cannot believe you really hit me!"

"I told you to get out of my face, and I meant it." There was no concern, no sorrow, nothing. As a matter of fact, she looked blank as if she could do it again. I felt the back of my head, and my fingers were covered with blood. I asked her if she would take a look at it, and she said no.

"Please see if I need stitches," I insisted.

"Next time you'll listen to me, won't you?" she remarked.

No matter what, I could not get her to look at the back of my head, even with all the blood that was on my hand. So I called my mom and dad's house. My sister was there, getting ready to turn in for the night. She told me to hurry up and get over there so she could get to bed. When I arrived, she said, "Oh, my gosh! What happened?" I told her, and she was ready for the bell to ring.

Realizing what I'd just said, I changed my story really quick. I told her that I'd fallen backward and hit my head on the table. My sister kept going back and questioning me about why I had first told her that it was my girlfriend and a coffee cup. "I don't know why," I would say. "I got tripped up, fell backward, and hit my head on the table."

After a while, the bleeding stopped, and I went back home. Sharon did not seem concerned at all. Thinking back on it now, I thank God for the handle breaking off that cup because there's no telling how much worse it would have been.

* * * * *

The other dealer, Jeremy, asked if he and his girlfriend, Karen, could rent a room from us. Things were looking good to me because the dope would be right there, and we wouldn't have to go chase it down, so they moved in.

Things were going great except everyone started to suspect the others of talking about them. It didn't matter who it was—there was even a time that I could have sworn the others were talking about me. It got so bad that I would eavesdrop on their conversations. When I got a hold on it, Sharon started, except that she would go up to Jeremy's door while it was closed and listen to him and Karen.

"Stop!" I would insist. "Why are you doing that?"

She would look at me and put her hand to her mouth to shush me. "Be quiet! I can't hear what they're saying."

This would go on for a while. Even Jeremy went through something similar, and Karen could have sworn that Sharon and I were talking about her. She asked multiple times about it. Even when Sharon was not around, she would ask, "Are you sure that y'all weren't talking about me?" When I assured her that we weren't, she would make me promise that I was telling the truth.

During all this time, I would be taking Jeremy places because he didn't have a car. That was okay with me because it just meant more pay for us in the form of dope. As time would carry on, I even got to where I would let him use my car to run errands and make deals.

One night, while it was just me and Sharon at home, there was this horrible, disgusting smell that I had noticed a handful of times, even at her place. I had tried so many ways to get an answer about it from different people, but the answers I got were not right. This time, I didn't say anything to her; I just went and took a shower.

Things continued on pretty much the same, except Sharon's pill use was back into full swing. We seemed to be fighting all the time over the stupidest stuff. Through it all, people started showing up, and we stayed in the den. Del came along and brought a friend, Dwayne. While they were there, Sharon had the radio up so loud that we couldn't talk. Dwayne came into the den with us. He fixed himself up a good shot and gave Sharon some. She looked at me and said, "He gave it to me, and I'm not sharing it with you."

I sat in there for a little while and finally announced, "I'm going to bed." No sooner had I laid my head down when the radio got turned down, and I could hear them talking. I couldn't take it anymore. I got up, walked into the den, and the radio got turned back up. I turned back around and hardly got into my room when the radio got turned back down again. So once again, I went back in there, and Sharon said, "I thought you were going to bed."

"Nope," I answered. "I decided to stay up." I sat right down there with them because I wasn't stupid. Between the amount of dope Dwayne had done, and my girlfriend the way she was, I didn't trust either one of them.

* * * * *

Again, that horrible, disgusting smell just kind of appeared while we had a house full of people. It didn't just gradually come on, I mean, it suddenly appeared. Well, there was no sense asking anyone there because they always gave the same answers. "It's the dope coming out of our skin," or, "When the dope is gone, the house will go back to the way it was." Of course, when I would question that, they'd say, "Nothing, don't worry about it. It will be okay."

A few days later, there was a knock at the door. It was Dwayne, the dealer's friend, the one who had given Sharon the dope. As soon as he came in, I asked, "Do you smell that horrible smell?"

"Yes."

"Well, what is it?"

"Someone's making meth in your house."

I went *crazy* looking everywhere. I searched in all the rooms, closets, garage, washer, dryer, and even under the house—nothing. Well, apparently, that wasn't the correct answer, so now I still didn't understand why that smell would just appear.

I had another question for Dwayne. I had started to see these insect-like things forming in a certain place. There were probably five or six of them. I had found them in other places in the house, different sizes, some of them much bigger than others. The ones that I found on the floor kind of reminded me of a giant mealworm because it only had legs toward the front of it, and they looked exactly the same every time. I'm guessing they were about five inches and were similar to the shape of an egg. Each one would also be lying flat with its head on the outside, and the last inch of it would always have a bend in it, kind of reminding me of a hook.

You see, I had noticed these insect-like creatures a couple of weeks prior and did not say anything to anyone because I believed they would say it was my imagination, it was not real, or I was crazy. So I showed him, putting my trustworthy flashlight beam on it. Right away, he saw it and immediately gave it a name—a meth bug. That was one answer I could accept. A couple of days passed, and my so-called girlfriend that loved me so much came up to me and questioned what I had asked Dwayne about. When I told her, she said that he was just playing with me. Within a couple of days, for some reason, the so-called meth bugs disappeared, but they left some of the parts where they had been attached to the wall.

One day, everyone left, and I got bored, so I came up with the brilliant idea of gathering up the tiny pieces of aluminum foil out of the carpet where I had once worked with it in the den. The pieces were so small that I used my knife and a spoon to pick them up. While I did this, I decided to collect the pieces in a small plastic container with a lid. Again why or even how I came up with this so-called brilliant idea, I really don't know. As I collected the aluminum foil fragments, I looked up and noticed there was a single fragment on the end table. As I went to pick it up, it moved—just enough to where I actually missed it.

I thought, *No way! There is no way that piece of aluminum foil moved the way it did to escape me picking it up.* I looked on my fingers to see if there might have been a hair or piece of fuzz stuck to my finger that may have moved it just in the nick of time. Well, nothing was on my finger. I looked at the table, but the table was made of dark wood, so of course, I didn't see anything that would have caused it to move the way it did. So again, I went to pick it up, moving slowly to see if it would happen again. This time, the aluminum foil fragment *allowed* me to pick it up. I held it up, looking at it very carefully, trying to get an answer for what I had just witnessed. I ended up just accepting that there was something on the table or on my finger that had caused it to move the way it did, so I just blew it off. In the back of my mind, though, I still wanted an answer.

I went back to work, collecting fragments for however long; it was a while because I had a pile of them in the container. I was actually amazed by the collection, kind of shaking it in the container and watching it, thinking of how it kind of reminded me of *glitter*. Then I heard car doors, so that meant that my roommates had gotten home. That also meant that I needed to move as fast as I could, putting everything away so they wouldn't make fun of me or tell me that I was crazy. I stashed the container in one of my dresser drawers under some clothes so nobody would find it.

A couple of days later, when I was in my room, something told me to check on the aluminum foil fragments that I had collected and make sure that they were still there. When I got them and looked at them, they had changed colors. Boy, was I baffled because they had been silver when I put them in the container. There was now a yellow tint to them. Again, to my amazement, I could not believe my eyes at what I was actually seeing. It was just another link in the chain of things I could not explain.

CHAPTER 10

One day, Sharon started shooting up part of a pill and decided to save some for later. Believe it or not, she was actually being nice to me, so I thought I'd take advantage of the opportunity and try to fool around. Afterward, she murmured, "I believe I'm going to finish my pill."

Within seconds, Sharon looked at me with this scared expression and lay down on the bed in a fetal position. I asked her if she was okay, but she was *not* herself—her voice was even different. I lay down beside her, realizing that something bad was going on.

When I put my arms around her, I could feel her cringing. I mean, she was scared to death of me. I really thought that she believed I was going to hurt her. I was really concerned about what was going on. After a little while, Sharon snapped out of it, and we went about our business. To this day, I really think that was not her. Question: What had happened?

* * * * *

One night, Jeremy and his friend, Dwayne, came storming into the house shouting, "They're here, they're here!"

"What do you mean?" I asked them.

"The agents are here!" Jeremy cried. "They're fixing to come in on us."

He explained that they'd been staying at a motel when the agents had raided and started questioning everybody. "What are we going to do?" he begged Dwayne. "My guns are out in the car. We need to go get them."

They ran outside and returned immediately, saying, "They're here, I saw them!"

I looked out the peephole of the door and saw nothing. "How do you know they're here?"

"I saw flashlights everywhere!" replied Jeremy.

I started freaking out. I thought that it was over and that I was fixing to go to jail.

Then, Jeremy looked at the dude and said, "We need to make a plan so we can get away."

They loaded their guns, and I was thinking, *What am I going to do if guns start going off?* I finally decided that if I lay down when the poop hit the fan, just maybe I wouldn't get hit by a bullet because I knew that I *was not* ready to die.

As they were getting ready for everything to unfold, Jeremy and Dwayne started talking about running for it. Let me tell you that Sharon was *all* up for that. She wanted to go with them so badly. Then I butted in, "No, you can stay here with me."

When they got ready to leave, Sharon started to go with them. "You need to stay!" Jeremy ordered as they slipped out the door.

They made their getaway in the car, but the agents never showed up at the house. The next day, Jeremy showed up, but nothing was ever brought up. I believe that it was the day after that when Karen asked if we'd heard what had happened. She told us that the motel everyone was at got raided. There were three rooms rented, and it just so happened that the room Jeremy and Dwayne were in didn't get busted on. That part of the story may have been true, and there may have been reason to panic, but the agents never busted in at my house.

* * * * *

A few days later, when everyone was gone, I was in my room and had noticed these cocoon-like things on the floor. They were almost all the exact same size. The more I looked, the more I found.

I could not understand why. Then again, I didn't want to ask. I felt like everyone was babysitting me, so I had to be careful not to get "in trouble," even though it was (and still is) my house. When they got home, I asked Sharon to please come to our room because I had something to show her. When she got there, I showed her the cocoons, and of course, it was nothing.

I began to look for something maybe different because I knew something was really going on. Then I found something—this was going to be one of the *biggest* discoveries of my forty-seven years on this place called earth. It was remarkable beyond words. It was a creature about as big as a marble: a brain with two eyes connected to it. A strain of woven fibers joined the two eyes with the brain connected in the middle. It was perfect, I mean a scientist or artist could never even do a replica. I picked it up, beyond baffled, and showed it to Sharon. Let me tell you, for once in my relationship with this woman, I had never seen her look so puzzled. I could see that her mind was racing, jumping mountains, and digging ditches. She was speechless, something I had never, ever seen.

All of a sudden, she snapped back from that place of shock and took the creature out of my hand. "It's not real!"

I didn't understand why she said that, so later on that day, after everyone was gone, I went back to the bedroom to try to figure out what the heck was going on. In other words, I wanted an answer, I needed an answer, and somehow, I was going to get an answer. It might be today, tomorrow, or maybe next year, but I *wanted that answer* almost more than anything. So I got to our room and began looking for the cocoons, but the ones that I had thrown back on the floor were gone. I began looking all over. They seemed to have disappeared again, another magic trick—*poof*—gone. I got to thinking that Sharon had probably done something with them.

Something told me to go look in the bathroom trash can. Wouldn't you know that whatever told me to look there was right; but at the time, I didn't care much because underneath the trash, there it all was. I began to gather it up to examine it and noticed that some of the cocoons had what appeared to be one green eye or maybe a brain. I just know that what I was looking at was unexplainable.

60

Then I heard the front door—panic mode time—so I took what I had in my hand and threw it under my bed.

* * * * *

During this time, as Jeremy and Karen were borrowing my car, I noticed that my car was changing. The inside just wasn't the same. I mean, literally, the vehicle seemed to be different somehow. Seriously, I knew my car. I'd had it for around five years, driving it almost every day, so how could I be wrong about something like that? When I asked for an explanation, I got different answers, but the one thing I knew was that all those answers were either lies, or my so-called friends just wanted to hide the truth. I was playing the game that I felt was being played because I wanted to know what was really going on.

So one night, after they had borrowed my car, they didn't come home. I called and called but no answer. I was scared of what might have happened to them and to my car. Finally, I got a break. Someone came by and said that they could have sworn that they had seen my car sitting in the parking lot of a motel. Thank God for spare keys— *here we go.*

Yes, there it is—my car! I felt relief well up in my body. When I got out to look it over, everything seemed to be intact. I did notice that there was a gas can in the backseat, so when I opened the car door, gas fumes almost knocked me down. I checked the gas can, and sure enough, there was gas in it. The can held one gallon, but it barely had half a gallon in it, probably closer to a quarter. Sharon and I rolled the windows down and let the car air out for a minute then jumped in the car and took off.

At this point in time, I really did not care what Jeremy and Karen thought. I didn't even care how in the heck they got back home. They'd said they'd be back but didn't have the decency to call me—after all, I had two phones. Not only that, but trust me, I wore their phones out trying to get them to answer.

When Sharon and I got back home, I took a good look at my car. I could see the transformation that I thought I'd been noticing all along. The inside really looked strange: there was stuff all over the seats, and the windshield had a clear milky film that looked like it had been both splashed and squirted on. The interior did not look the same, and the carpet on the floorboard seemed like it was doing what it was doing in my bedroom—rolling up.

When they got home, I asked Jeremy why I couldn't get ahold of them. I can't really remember exactly what his excuse was, but the more I think on it, I can almost swear that he said that they'd run out of gas or someone they knew had run out. But how come there was some gas left in the can? It didn't make sense.

Then, I asked about what happened to the inside of my car, and I know this quote is accurate: "What do you mean? Your car is the same as when we left. You don't know what you're talking about." *No way, this is crazy*, I thought. *I know what I see, and they are full of an extra-large truckload of bull poop!*

Anyway, Jeremy was a dealer, and dealers can find a way anywhere. All it takes is a phone call and letting that person know that he has something for them—and *bingo*—like magic, that person usually drops what they're doing to pick up the dealer for their so-called payment.

Trust me, I know because I have been that person many times. I have given rides, transported drugs, gone grocery shopping, cooked, cleaned, made deliveries, and even mowed yards. The one thing that I can say that I never did was sexual favors. Some people will do anything for another fix, and sexual favors are common, especially with girls. Depending upon what they look like and how bad their addiction is, most girls will do almost anything, and I mean *anything* for their dope.

I never personally witnessed any of these acts because that was *beyond disgrace*. It's bad enough to look at yourself and not only see that you have a problem because I *knew* I did. I just *could not* get a hold of myself because of my addiction. Excuse me for putting it to you like this, but the most truthful way to say it is that, throughout my life, my addiction literally had me by the balls.

Anyway, I knew all these things were true. Listening to certain girls and listening to certain dealers, I'd hear them tell each other stories and hear them laugh about what certain girls did just for one hit. A couple of times, I even took this one woman to meet a client of hers so she could perform sexual acts for him. Then I would get a call to come pick her up. Trust me, the payment—which was dope and gas money if I needed it—was always good.

There would be times throughout my life, being addicted to whatever, that I did not have money. I would call around, trying to find some way to make me some dope (payment). In the dope world, a lot of times, they call this *work*.

Let me give you my definition of work on this side:

> *Work*, trying not to get caught by the police when you are getting low on product/ dope. Getting more because whoever needs a fix will go somewhere else if you don't have what they need.

If someone goes somewhere else to get their fix, then you are taking a chance of the other guy's dope being better than yours. They might even give the client a little extra just to make sure they come back. Most important is the money—money that you will miss out on or the dope that you yourself will miss out on for your fix (addiction)!

Addiction can hit anyone, and *I mean anyone!* I personally witnessed Jeremy (the dealer who was still staying with me) give his parents shots and drugs. I had thought that they'd already had a problem and he'd been helping them out. Time told the truth, though, he was the one who got them hooked on meth/ice. So not only is it the mothers, fathers, or the people you hang out with; this proves that drugs are not prejudiced. They entice you into trying them so you will get addicted. Drugs are designed to take you down their road. That road is fun in the beginning until it has you. Then it will take you to the *dead end* that is six feet deep.

CHAPTER 11

One day, Jeremy took off with someone, and a few hours later, he came home with a vehicle that he had bought. I liked it—it was a little sports car. Little by little, he began to put money into his stereo system. The next thing I knew, I could hear him coming from a mile away. I live in a nice subdivision that is pretty quiet, and the neighbors respect each other. But of course, being who he was, it was all about him and "Who cares what anyone else thinks?"

In other words, he seemed to think that he was the only one who counted. No, I knew it didn't work like that because I respected my neighbors. Many times did I meet him outside as he was pulling up to remind him to turn down the loud music. Then he got to where he would go outside just to jam. The music would be so loud that I swear the house would shake—really, the windows would vibrate! This guy had no respect. It *did not* matter what time of day, night, or even morning.

There really is no such thing as time when you are deep into this drug, except time to re-up (getting more work/drugs). When you've been up for days, why worry about time? Life becomes all about getting high and partying; it's a way of life.

The longest that I was ever up was eight or nine days but usually just a few days at a time. Then it would be—*crash*—pass out, just fall asleep, and wake up wherever that might be. Depending upon how long you have been up, you might sleep for days. I know someone that supposedly had been up for thirty-six days! I believe it because toward the end, I never saw him sleep. He was taking shots that would have put an elephant on its knees. To top it off, if you ever talked to him, you would never know that he was on anything—he was very smart with a college education.

* * * * *

What is the saying? "You are supposed to learn from your mistakes." Okay, does that mean me too? After the Florida trip, I swore that I would never, ever go back there again with Sharon. Wait, I said *Florida*, right? Her family wanted us to go to Myrtle Beach, South Carolina, with them. That didn't count, right? Because it wasn't Florida?

When Sharon invited me to go, I told her that I'd sworn to myself that I'd never take a trip of any sort with her again. She started saying that this one would be different. She swore that we would take a walk on the beach and actually be a couple.

Well, that started sounding like maybe it might not be so bad. Let me use another saying: "People tell you what you want to hear to get what they want." We had no money (imagine that), and her mom, of all people, called and asked if Sharon would come down to the beach because it was her mom's birthday, and she missed her. To me, that translated to, "I could use more money, and if you come, then the trip will be paid for. Then when I get home, I can make even more money off the stuff that you steal for me and the pills that you buy off me. *Yeah, money!*"

Let me use yet another saying before I carry on: "Love is blind." That said I kind of understood, but it never took hold. As for today, my eyes are opened, and, boy, do I see the light.

So it was Sheila's birthday, and she had Sharon go to her niece's to get money so we could have gas to get there. Sheila promised to pay her niece back when she arrived because she was planning to join us in a couple of days. Sounds great, does it not? So when Sharon got the money, she wanted to get a little dope. I had asked her how that was possible, and let me tell you, she had it all worked out, knowing exactly to the dime how much money we would need. Think about it—she had done this trip many, many times.

We got our dope, went back home, and started getting high, knowing that we were already a couple of hours behind. When we finally got on the road, we needed gas really bad. That was when I was introduced to "pump and jump." That means to go to a gas station, get out, stand by the car, and wait for them to turn on the pump. If they do, then pump the gas, jump back in the car, and leave as fast as possible. That was crazy because I *do not* do things like that. I was a nervous wreck. I just knew that we were going to get caught. Sharon kept laughing at me, saying that it was going to be okay.

We got down the road a good poke then stopped at another gas station. She told me to sit in the car, and she would be right back; this was what she did all the time, but still, I never got used to it. She would fill her pocketbook full of junk food so we'd have something to eat. Moving on again, we got so far down the road and decided to finish our dope. So we got off at the next exit, driving along—not stopping—and finished it.

I was driving, and when we got back on the interstate, I began to see things that kind of reminded me of people. When we would get close to whatever it was, it would become something else. This made no sense. I can say for once that I thought I was tripping. (Then again, think about it—seeing people that turned out to be something else—does that sound like maybe something I've talked about before?)

Further down the road, Sharon started saying, "We're in trouble because we're about out of gas, and the next gas station is too far away."

So once again, I was in panic mode, thinking, *How freaking stupid can I get? I knew better than to go on this trip!* The car began sputtering. It was looking very, very bad for the home team, and yes, I was stuck on this team because I *picked* it. It got to the point that when we would get enough speed, Sharon would turn the car off and coast, doing this over and over.

After what seemed to be all night, there was a literal sign of hope: a road sign that there was a gas station up ahead! The only problem was that the car did not want to run. I mean, have you ever heard the phrase "running on fumes"? I promise that fumes were what kept us going. When we got to the exit, there was a little hill. We coasted down that hill all the way till we got to the pumps. When we arrived, I begged, "Please let me go in and pay for the gas."

Sharon gave me twenty dollars. "This is it, so we better be able to make it."

Well, we made it, but no one would answer the phone. We went and found a place to park. As we were talking, I could have sworn that there were people all around, but there never was anybody. It was like I would see them, but they would never come around.

The sun began to break. There were some clouds, but I could still see the sunrise, and let me tell you, it was beautiful. The people I thought I'd been seeing were nowhere around. Finally, Sharon's mom answered her phone, and we were on our way to breakfast. A couple of Sheila's friends came along, much younger than we were, and Sharon was good with them.

After we got back from breakfast, I went to watch the waves and listen to them crash into the beach. (Of course, I was by myself.) When I got back, it was time to go shopping. By *shopping*, I mean Sheila and her friends picking things out and my girlfriend boosting (stealing).

We got back, rested, and started all over again. The thing was, Sharon started to get sick because her mom didn't bring her kind of drugs, so she was wanting to find some. Me being the person that I was, I could find drugs. Trust me, I could find drugs. So going out to the car, I noticed this guy. I *knew* what, so I went up to his SUV and began talking. Then he said the magic words, "Do you need anything?"

I started telling him what was up then asked Sharon to come over. "Tell him what you want."

We started talking about products and prices. She explained that I was taking her to boost and asked him if there was anything he wanted. After we got back, the dude was nowhere around. Things were looking rough because she was getting very pill-sick.

The next night, following another day of "shopping," I noticed these guys in a store parking lot. *There it is,* I thought to myself. *I can smell the drugs.* Not really, but the way they were acting and carrying themselves, I knew that it was going to be a home run. *Perfect!*

One dude came by the car, and I said, "What's up?"

He looked at me. "What's up?"

Yes, I had found the winning ticket.

He leaned in my car. "Are you the police? What do you need?"

I told him to get into the car, and he started pulling out all kinds of drugs: cocaine, crack, and heroin. Sharon came out of the store and got his number. What a mistake that was going to be. To make a long story short, we did make it to the beach. Believe it or not, we even swam in the ocean. After that, though, I was the most horrible person in the whole universe. Sheila's friends weren't any help because if they opened their mouths, they wouldn't get any drugs. She had been feeding them pills, and they had no money, so I was by myself. It was so bad that the drug dealer saw what was going on and actually hooked me up with some crack. Then everyone took off again.

This group of young people went walking by, and one guy came up to me. He offered me a cigarette then asked if I was okay. This was astounding—someone actually cared. I didn't even know them; they were Christians.

It was almost daylight when everyone finally made it back. Attitudes were the same. It went from bad to worse—my car started overheating. It took a while to solve the problem, but we survived. On our way home, disaster struck again, and we had a flat.

Then, my luck jumped from my car to their friend's car. The girls called my phone saying that they were going to run out of gas and that Sheila wouldn't answer the phone. So I called her. "It's not my fault, and I can't do anything," she grumbled. "They should have saved enough money."

I told Sharon what her mom said. The girls started calling back, and Sharon hissed, "Don't answer the phone, turn it off or they will keep calling!" Boy, that did not make me feel terrible. Even though they didn't help me, I still felt bad for them. They never did get Sheila to bring them gas money, but to my knowledge, they're still friends to this day. Why not? They like pills, and Sharon's mom is a pill dealer.

* * * * *

We finally made it home and intercepted some meth/ice. A few days later, we made a delivery for the dealer. As we were leaving, I noticed that my car was overheating again. I began to look for water, but Sharon kept insisting, "It will be okay, we'll make it."

Even though I should have known better, we took off. We were on the interstate climbing a mountain, which pushed the car even harder. The engine started sputtering. I turned to look out the back window and saw nothing but smoke. *Big problem!* There was nowhere to pull over because there was a retaining wall on both sides of the road. *Keep pushing,* I told myself. *Can't stop now!*

Finally, there was a place to pull over, and surprisingly, the car was still running. I turned it off, so that was a plus, but it was pretty obvious my car had completely bit the dust. I called Jeremy to come get us, and while we waited, I commented to Sharon, "Well, you won't be around long because I can't take you where you need to go."

Her reply was, "You think so."

Things began looking up because we were able to use the dealer's car every day for a few hours. After a week or two, though, his brakes started getting bad. He didn't want us to drive his car because of the danger.

With nothing to do and nowhere to go, I fell asleep in the bed for once, waking up to Sharon doing dope. She had been up all night, shooting up and doing pills. As my head cleared from the sleep, I realized Sharon didn't seem normal; she didn't look or even sound like my girlfriend.

Sharon asked for my pipe. and I gave it to her. "Are you going to take me boosting?"

I didn't answer. She asked again, so I said, "Come here."

She finally came and sat on the bed. I was rubbing her back, murmuring, "You know I love you".

"I love you, too. Are you going to take me?"

I didn't know what to say because Jeremy didn't want us using his car.

Again, Sharon prodded, "Are you going to take me?" I just looked at her. She asked yet again then followed it by, "If you don't, you know that I can find a way."

She pressed a couple more times, and then there was a knock at the door. Guess who? Yes, it was Jeremy's friend, Dwayne.

I begged Sharon not to go, telling her that I would take her. "You had your chance."

I must have looked wary because the dude defended, "Man, I do not want your girlfriend! I'll bring her back after she's done."

Well, I called her phone many times, only to get an answer one time. After being gone all day, and I mean all day, Sharon came storming in, grabbing a few things and giving me a bunch of stuff. I knew that she was not coming back—she was lying, and I knew it.

I once asked my girlfriend why she would lie to me so much. She said, "When I tell you something, I really mean it at the time. I can't help the way things happen."

I don't understand how someone can "mean it," knowing they're going to change their mind. Some people might call that a "little white lie," but no matter how you look at it, it's still a lie.

Either way, we were done for good. I realized how bad all this made me feel. It was destroying me.

As I worked through the pain, it suddenly hit me—*now, I can finally get some answers.* This was something I had wanted for so long. The questions I had asked always led me nowhere, and the answers people gave always fell short. I began to look around for whatever, looking for a change, looking to solve the question, to *find the answer.*

This is where the rubber meets the road.

CHAPTER 12

Things were changing. I couldn't really explain it; I just knew that they were. The one thing that I did know was that I really loved the night. I mean, I looked forward to it—the dark. When darkness would come, I was almost excited; then daybreak would come, and it was disappointing. Still, the one thing that I could count on was going outside after dark and watching the shadow people. They would be in the same places almost every time. There were always four or five of them a couple of houses down from me between the neighbor's truck and the wooden fence. Then there would be at least one, maybe two, that would run across the yard on the next street. And of course, there were always those that just stood around doing nothing but making sure that I saw them.

Then, one night, it was different. I looked out the window of the house and saw something that just seemed to call me outside. I went to the road and began to move very slowly like I was sneaking. Looking up beside the policeman's house, on the other side of his car, I saw three men standing there watching my house. I stared at them for a long time, watching for movement. One of them had coveralls on. That registered with me because I was wearing shorts, and I knew that they had to have been *really* hot. The whole time I watched them, I never saw them move.

The policeman came outside and went down to the road, carrying something. Then he went to his car and opened the door. The three men seemed to have gotten in, but had they really moved that fast? Something didn't look right. Let me tell you that when the policeman's lights came on, they were aimed right at me and my house, and if I ever moved fast, this time I moved like a streak of lightning.

A little later, I was drawn outside again, looking for the three men because I could have sworn they *did not* get in the policeman's car. I was thinking that just maybe they hadn't seen me, and I might be able to find them.

Something caught my eye up the road. There was someone on the side of the road just standing there. I went across the street to the neighbor's house, leaning up against its corner, watching the person near the road. As I kept my eye on them, they would not move. Then the person would turn into a mailbox, then turn into a person, then a mailbox again.

Suddenly, two more men appeared just up from the person—I mean, the mailbox—I mean, person—no, really, it *was* a mailbox! Or was it? I could still imagine seeing a person there. They started across the road. It looked as if there were lots of people where they were headed.

As I watched, this little light caught my eye, moving from one side of the house to the other. I noticed it would come back to the same place it started. The light would take the same route that it took before and then do it all over again. Then the same two men crossing the road would catch my eye, appearing just like the light. (The reason I knew that it was the same people was that one had an orange shirt.)

I have no idea how long I stayed there watching, but I noticed this one person who stood very cocked—I mean, kind of like a forty-five-degree angle. Other than that, they looked normal from the feet to the hips. That one really kept me watching because I knew a person that actually stood like that when they would get high.

See, there were phases that people would go through that were crazy, myself included, like making these groaning sounds. Then smoking—if a person developed that habit, they'd have something in the back of their throat that seemed to really hang on, and if they ever got it out, almost instantly—*bingo*—it was back, making the person want to choke, driving them crazy. Then something might be wrong with their nose. It seemed as if something was growing out of it.

As for me, I would feel something strange in my nose. I would take my finger and sometimes my knife and dig up in there. Then I would forget about it, then I would feel it. It actually seemed to be climbing up the outside of my nose, reminding me of a tree root on the ground when I looked at it in the mirror. Let me tell you that I knew that whatever it was, *it was growing*. One time, I took my knife and began really digging, making sure that whatever I did, I would get this thing taken care of once and for all. I made it hurt. Whatever it was, it was coming out. It was not buried on the inside of my nose, but let me tell you that it had a grip! It *did not* want to leave where it was located.

Then, down in my personal place, it would kill me. Sometimes, when I went to sit down, it felt like I was getting scratched inside. All these things that would happen happened to everybody that did ice—if not exactly the same way, then similar. They called it a phase; it was supposed to be normal. I guess no matter what the phase was, it was torture. Then again, I was addicted to this drug. I realized that I would have to go through the phases, so I made up my mind to put on my big boy panties and make the bed that I was lying in because I was not quitting. I was supposed to be having so much fun; this nightmare of addiction.

* * * * *

One night, I was back at my house looking for change with my flashlight when something told me to look in the shoes. Funny—*something* kept telling me to look in certain places, and lo and behold, I would find things. The shoes were on a rack about three feet off the ground and had not been worn in a long time. I took a closer look and noticed that something seemed different on the inside of the shoes. I could not believe my eyes. There it was—another cocoon-like creature!

I had found something like this before, but when I put it in a zipper-sealed bag, I accidentally killed it because it had suffocated. This one was similar—like a rice cake, perfectly round. *No way, this is impossible. How can this thing be in this shoe, standing straight up?*

This creature was hairy, just like the other one. As I looked closer, I noticed the hairs were moving in a wave. I felt as if it was wanting me to get it out of the shoe, so I knocked the shoe on the table, and it came out. *It likes me! It is my friend.* I picked it up, inspecting it even closer, and saw all the cocoons that it was made of. I was not scared of it; I felt as if I had a new friend or a pet. *I need to go put him under my bed where he will be safe,* I reasoned.

As a couple of days carried on, I would check on my so-called friend. I noticed that it was changing, taking another form, so then I started calling it an egg. I also noticed that the one I had accidentally killed had begun to take form, actually rising up off the carpet.

The cocoons that had been under the bed were gone, but I noticed that there were even more cocoons on the floor through-out my room. What I found next was baffling. There were these little green cocoons that were lined up in two rows, staggered per-fectly. Each one was about the size of a bee. You see, what was baf-fling about the little green cocoons was that there was nothing green around there. A couple of weeks before that, there had been a green blanket there that I had put up in my closet. *No way!* I thought. *This is not possible—but then again, it has to be because I know the difference between real and not real.*

I began to speed up the process by picking up the cocoons and putting them under the bed. Then I would put them in specific places so I could prove that I was not crazy; I *needed* to know the answer to what was going on. I would check the cocoons throughout the day, noticing that nothing would happen. Then night would come about, and let me tell you that it would happen—almost everything that I would put in specific places would—*poof*—magically appear under my bed.

* * * * *

One day, in the hall, something passed by me. I turned really quickly to look at whatever it was. I didn't see anything, but I knew that something had been there. When it happened again, I could see just enough of it to *know* exactly what it was. God's honest truth, there was *no doubt*—it was a shadow person. It didn't bother me or even scare me because I said to it, "It's a shadow person, it's my friend."

I started getting some answers about what was going on, just not the *complete truth*. In other words, I was being blinded to the truth, the light, the *real answer*—the answer they did not want me to know. I was in my bedroom, checking under my bed, looking at the things there still changing, taking form. As I searched, I started to get this feeling that something bigger was going on. Could it be God? I paused for a moment. Then I declared, "God is our Father, Jesus is my Savior, and the Holy Spirit I *love*, but the dark side I hate. I will accept any gift that you want to give me—bring it on."

CHAPTER 13

Things kept manifesting in strange ways. There would be that terrible smell again—disgusting, horrifying. The smell always seemed to appear at night, but where did it come from?

One day, I was walking by the hall bathroom, and again, something told me to look in there. When I walked in and began looking for some reason to search, I was drawn to the trash can. As I picked it up to look inside, I could not believe my eyes. *How can this be real?* It was the exact same egg thing that I had found in the trash can months before. It even had a piece of plastic sticking out of it. This time, I did not hesitate; I grabbed it, took it straight to my room, and threw it under my bed.

Again, this thing I called an egg was perfectly round and probably about the exact same size as a rice cake. It was about four inches long and an eighth of an inch thick, and of course, it too was hairy. After a couple of hours, I was getting excited thinking about it and decided to go check on it. Lo and behold, the new egg that I threw under my bed was perfectly upright, standing right beside the other one. *What is going on here?* I wondered. *There is no possible way that it landed like that.*

At home alone again one day, I was bored. *What can I do?* Then an idea came to me. I decided to cut out the bottom of the couch liner and see if I could find any dope that might have been dropped. After I got done there, I started on the parts of the couch where anything could have gotten trapped. I found a few things, so I started separating everything by category. Before it was over, I had probably three different piles. One of the piles consisted of very small fragments of aluminum foil.

The foil fragments became a challenge to me. Some nights, when I was bored, I would grab a spoon, get the flashlight out of my pocket, and go collect aluminum foil fragments. They were so small that they had worked their way down into the carpet. Jeremy and Karen were in their bedroom one night, so I went into the den and turned on my flashlight. There on top of the carpet was a small piece of foil. When I went to get it, it disappeared into the carpet. *What?* I wondered. There was another piece sticking up, so when I went to get that one, it too disappeared. How could those aluminum foil fragments just disappear like that?

I put my flashlight in my mouth and started pulling the carpet apart. I found one of the foil fragments, but when I went to get it, it disappeared. *Boy, am I like messed up, or what?* Then I found another piece, and it too was—*poof*—gone. After about four or five tries, I actually got a piece trapped between the spoon and knife. *Okay,* I thought, *I could have sworn that I saw it wiggle as I had it trapped between the spoon and knife.* So I put that piece of foil up with the pieces that I had collected from the couch liner. Well, I was successful a few more times, but I came to the conclusion that those foil fragments were running from me.

Then, my roommate's door opened, and I jumped up on the couch, just sitting there. Jeremy came walking by, looked at me, and said that he was going to the store and would be right back. When he got home, he gave me a couple of doughnuts and went back to his room. By this time, it was a little after daylight. I was looking for an answer to what was going on with the aluminum foil, so I started to examine the pieces on the table. As I went to touch one of them, I could have sworn that it moved. When I tried again, it did the same thing, but I *did not* stop there. I picked it up and looked at it, wondering what the heck was going on.

For some reason, I dropped it on the carpet. It was amazing, I mean, it was magic—the piece of aluminum foil disappeared into the carpet! So I did it again, and the same result—*magic!* I did this over and over until I took the remaining pieces and dropped all of them on the floor, again, watching all the pieces disappear into the carpet. *No way!*

Boy, let me tell you that my mind was traveling so fast that I'm pretty sure I broke the speed of sound if at all possible, trying to get an answer for what was going on. Then I remembered that I had played with foil in my bedroom, so I decided to go in there to see if just maybe I could find more fragments in there. Looking around my room, I couldn't find any, but then I looked under my bed. There it was!

I went to touch one fragment, and it turned and looked at me. I *could not* believe my eyes—it was not scared of me. Then it disappeared into the carpet. As if I was not baffled enough, it came back up again and looked at me!

I know you all are thinking, *Looking at you? How can an aluminum foil look at you?* Let me take it a step further and ask you: How can whatever is going on even *happen*? But it did, and this foil fragment was like a person. It had eyes that looked like something out of cartoons.

I searched some more and found a couple more foil people, and they too would also be what I called friendly. Of course, then there was the question as to why one was friendly and the other tried to get away because I always needed answers to my questions.

The answer came to me in the den. We had company, and there were people walking around in there. I got to think about what would happen if the foil got stepped on. I remembered that when I would go to pick it up, the movement caused it to take cover in the carpet. Now the aluminum foil that was under my bed had no traffic; therefore, it would not take cover. By patting the carpet under the bed, though, it would aggravate the foil to the point that it would disappear but soon come back up.

About that time, I met this man and woman, and we became pretty good friends. As time went on, I finally trusted the guy enough to ask him to take a look. When I showed him the aluminum foil under my bed, he was amazed at what was going on. He even asked me, "How are you doing this?"

I showed his wife, and she actually said that there was a lot of *energy* in my room. I did not know what she meant, but it sounded good to me. *Let's go with that answer,* I thought. *At least I have an answer.* To tell you the truth, the husband only came into my room one more time, and as for the wife, she never went into my room again. *Huh,* I reasoned. That must have really been some energy because they continued to come over but avoided my "energized" room.

I started finding these figurines of all kinds: people, dogs, geese (*geese* is what I called them because those particular ones had long necks). There were also monsters, demons, and things that I called demon angels that were snakes with a single wing on each side. As I would find these figurines, I would show people at the house, and almost every time, they would say, "Cool! How did you make that?"

Now, think, I never said anything, just showed them to prove to myself that what I was seeing was real and that I was not crazy. So just like the aluminum foil fragments under the bed, there were aluminum foil people and then these figurines. I got *validation* and knew that what I had been seeing was real. The question I have for them today is: Are you still blind to the truth, or can you see the light that is the only truth?

CHAPTER 14

From time to time, that horrible smell would reappear. To my surprise, I realized that I had started to like that smell because when that smell came, magical things would happen. I mean, the house would come to life!

There were those so-called eggs under my bed. I had five or six big things that were taking shape under with lots of small figurines. These were beginning to morph into a form like people, with the big ones wearing crowns on their heads. The people looked very mad as if they were super irritated which, at the same time, seemed funny to me.

Then, one night, I was alone and began the usual search for loose change or whatever I could find or even get into. As I was in one of the bedrooms, something told me to look under the bed. Let me tell you, I will never get this image out of my mind because when I first saw it, it scared the you-know-what out of me.

I lifted the skirt of the bed and saw insects—thousands of them. Their eyes were red with a pinkish tint that looked like they were glowing. The first thing I said was, "What are all these insects doing under this bed?"

They were looking directly at me, so I began to ask them questions. "What is that on your heads?" I didn't get an answer, but after a closer look, I realized that they were wearing crowns made of intricate fibers, strangely beautiful.

Then, I noticed the heat. The floor had become reddish-orange with goldish-silverish streaks running through it. "How is the bed not catching on fire?" I wondered. The heat waves were incredible coming off the floor.

The next day I went back and looked under the bed, everything was gone. Then again, why not?

* * * * *

I was bored. Sounds like trouble, but as ridiculous as it may sound, I needed a good way to get my mind off of the last *nightmare* that I'd seen. (At the time, it didn't seem like a nightmare, but knowing what I know today, it most certainly was and still is a nightmare in a way because of the memories and reliving it to write this book to bring the truth to you all.)

I don't remember what I was doing that night, but I do remember that I had folded a piece of aluminum foil into a small piece about the size of a nickel and about four high. For some reason, it was not thick enough, so I took another piece of foil and folded it in between. I got a hammer and a very small nail, trying to drive it through the foil, but the piece that was in the middle kept slipping out. *Why can I not keep this piece inside?*

Then, finally, I did it; I drove the small nail into the foil. As I looked at it, I became confused, thinking about the foil people and wondering if I might have hurt this folded piece of foil.

For some reason, I took it apart, pondering how it seemed to separate as I tried to drive the nail into it. Then I came up with an idea so that maybe I could get an answer to the question. I took two more pieces of foil: one was about the size of a nickel, and the other was smaller than a dime. I put the smaller one in the middle, trying to fold it. To my amazement, that task was not possible. Every time I would start folding the smaller one in between the two bigger ones, the smaller one would come scooting out across the palm of my hand. It just happened so fast.

I got to where I would not accept that this piece of foil was faster than I was, so I kept trying—getting faster and faster—while, at the same time, unfolding the larger foil to try to trap the smaller one inside. Needless to say, I was never successful. To tell you the truth, I don't believe that I even came anywhere close to succeeding.

As I studied it, I came up with a brilliant idea (which turned out to open up a whole new world of torture). Looking at the pieces of foil, puzzled, I got to wonder if they were moving, what would happen if I were to cut them into small pieces? So I started cutting them up, laying them in my hand, pressing the scissors flat against my palm. I kept cutting until I felt as if I could not get them any smaller. To tell you the truth, they actually looked like glitter. After I finished, I just stared at the pieces of foil, thinking that they were going to move, but of course, they did not. So I put the pile on my chest of drawers, thinking that this ordeal was over; but let me tell you, that was just the beginning.

While I was standing at my chest of drawers, I felt something crawling on me. I began to look myself over. I couldn't tell what it was, but I sure could feel it. Then I noticed that the glitter foil fragments had moved. The reason that I knew they had moved was that I had put them where I could not accidentally hit them and knock them over. When I realized that they had moved, I knew exactly what I was dealing with. I took my flashlight and started searching. There. There was the glitter, but it was no longer glitter. What I saw were foil spiders. *No way! How can this be possible?* All that glitter had turned into spiders, and they were after me!

Let me tell you that spiders and I *do not* get along. Depending upon the location of a spider, I can freak out. The next thing I knew, the foil spiders were in my head, driving me crazy. I mean, literally, I was going insane. I told Jeremy about the spiders, and then I captured as many as I could, putting them in a little tackle box that had one shelf inside it. I took a shipping tape and went around it so that whatever tried to climb out would get stuck. Then I put the tackle box under my bed because the foil spiders seemed to like the dark. By this time, it was daylight, and it looked like they were asleep.

A little while later, I checked on them. There were a few stuck to the tape, but not what I expected. So I just put them on top of my bed. I tried to show Jeremy, and he acted like he looked at them, but I know he didn't. By this time, my bed was covered with all kinds of experiments. In other words, when I looked at my bed, I could see *questions looking for answers*, not sleep, because when I went to sleep, it was wherever I crashed.

Then, it started back up—something was crawling on me again. I looked at the tackle box and realized that I had not put tape where the shelf was, and the next thing I knew, the spiders were back in my head, driving me insane. When I got things under control, I scraped up as many spiders as I could and put them in the toilet. Why I didn't flush, you tell me. Big mistake!

Later on that night, I was in the bathroom sitting on the toilet seat, doing experiments, trying to get answers. Then I felt something crawling on my legs. *What in the you-know-what is all over me?* Then it hit me, *no way!* I lifted up the seat, and the spiders were climbing out. They were climbing up the toilet bowl, and there were a couple of them on the rim.

Okay, I have had enough of this bull——! This is it, I will not make the same mistake twice! I was going to war, not realizing at the time that I was fighting a losing battle. After I thought that I had as many as possible, I flushed the little suckers and *did not* have any remorse about what I did because they were pure torture.

By the next night, I was really amazed. The foil spiders were *everywhere*. My room was not safe because everywhere I turned, there they would be. During daylight hours, they seemed to be asleep because they would not be on the attack or even move for that matter. So I came to the conclusion that I was safe during the daytime, but at night, I could not lean so much against anything to give them a jumpstart at making it into my head.

During this time, I had been showing Jeremy and Karen the foil people, which they said were not real. Then one day, Karen came up to me and admitted, "I have seen them. Why do you think I vacuum the den all the time? They freak me out!"

Jeremy continued to be in denial, so I made videos on my cell phone and showed them to him. Okay, if what I videoed was not real, then explain why he watched the whole video, still insisting, "I don't see nothing!"

It got to where Karen was cleaning almost every night. "Why are you cleaning your room so much?" I asked her.

The answer that I got was, "I wasn't cleaning." Well, that was a bald-faced lie.

"I was watching you!"

Still lying, she held her ground and never told the truth.

Then, one night, Karen and I were alone, and I was getting ready to lie down on a pile of clothes that were on the floor by the radio. As I was getting settled, I saw lots of foil spiders, so I immediately picked up the shirt on top of the pile. To top it off, the shirt was black, so the spiders showed up great. I went into their room to show Karen, but of course, she said she saw nothing.

"If there is *nothing* on this shirt," I told her, "I will shake it off on your bed!"

"You better not!"

"But if there's nothing on the shirt, then *why not?*" I challenged. "I will just lay the shirt down and leave it with you."

"You better not!" she repeated. "Take it with you!"

We went round and round again. I remember thinking that this had to be real because she wanted nothing to do with the shirt and *did not* want me to leave it in her room. In my mind, the question was answered by the way she acted. Karen knew it was real. She wanted no part of the shirt and wouldn't even touch it.

As time would carry on, it seemed as if the spiders were getting to where they were not after me anymore. I remember waking up on the floor one morning, and the spiders were all around me. I just looked at them, amazed at how many there were. I felt as if they were telling me that things were "even" between us, but at the same time, they were always there, like they were making sure that I never forgot who they were.

I swear the foil spiders were haunting me. No matter where I was in my room, there were always some around. When I would smoke dope, they would almost always be in my pipe; the pipe was glass, and I could see them. Even when I would get my dope ready to shoot up, almost every time there would be some crawling around in the spoon, crawling around on the filter that I would use to remove anything that was not supposed to get into the shot. That being said, they would sometimes get into the shot. How? I do not have a clue, but that was a pain in the butt because they did not want to come out.

I really wanted to know the truth. What's more, I wanted to know if Karen and Jeremy knew the truth about what all this was. Foil people, foil spiders—who knew?

One night, Karen was vacuuming, and she wandered into my room. Let me tell you, that was not a good decision. I almost came unglued, thinking that she was vacuuming up my friends. Before it was over, Karen never cleaned in my room again. A couple of days passed, and she came up to me and said that she had been joking about the foil people freaking her out and that she was just saying that. I was puzzled as to why she would come up to me out of the blue and tell me something like that. It's one thing to be blind to the light, but maybe it's possible to be blinded because something or someone tricked you, turned the light off, and it was total darkness—in other words, seriously lost beyond recognition.

CHAPTER 15

The smell was back. It was horrible, but it was also lovely because it meant excitement. It was dark and beautiful because of what it meant, and what it meant was one thing and one thing only.

I still watched the shadow people outside at night, trying to figure out what they were doing. In the process, some of them kind of liked to play games. I mean, it was like they wanted me to think that I was seeing things. Personally, I knew what they were to me—they were friends who I could always count on being outside every night if I was bored.

I did wonder where all the shadow people were when it was daylight because they were not outside during the day. Sometimes, there would be some inside my house during daylight hours, but they did not show themselves that much. One time, right before the sun came up, I watched one walk from the outside wall and go into the bathroom. It took a couple of steps and then—*poof*—like magic; it walked through the other wall.

Let me also remind you about the things under my bed—there were so many of them, and I really have no way to explain them. There were those eggs that changed into people who looked really angry. There were animals and insects that I have never seen before, people, and demon-like creatures. There was also a giant lizard-looking thing that I ended up calling a dragon because of all the demon-like things that were on its back. And of course, there were still all those so-called aluminum foil people everywhere. I kept everything organized. I had been putting certain things in certain places so that when I got bored, I knew where it all was. That way, I could go straight to whatever I wanted to play with.

In the meantime, I found this little battery (it was not even a half-inch long). I took it to my bedroom to see what would happen because if it was on my floor and was not too big, I knew it would come to life. So I put the battery down by the bedpost, next to my feet, where I knew it was. I checked on the battery, and nothing seemed to happen.

Then, night came.

I took my knife out and went to touch the battery, I guess to move it around, trying to figure out why it didn't seem to be working. As I went to touch it, the battery attacked my knife. *No way!* I tried it again. Right before my knife could even touch the battery, it would attack again, over and over. The noise that it would make was incredible like a crunching sound.

That opened up a door to me, wondering what the foil people would do with my knife. Let me tell you, this too was mind-boggling. I discovered that the foil people were not the same—they each had personalities. Some of them did not like the knife, some would turn and look at the knife, and then some would get scared and go down into the carpet but come back up very cautiously, trying to figure out what it was. There were even some that would attack the knife.

I went down the hall and noticed a small screw. *Bingo!* I thought. *I know exactly what to do with it.* The screw was not even a half-inch long, and I thought that it would be a good candidate as a friend for the battery. So I took it to my room and laid it beside the battery, watching to make sure that there was no fighting going on.

Fighting, did I say *fighting*? Let me say this again: with this drug, I don't care who you are, you will be fighting for some of the most ignorant stuff too baffling to explain. Meth kept me from being who I really was, but I never lost sight of *love*. I might have lost sight of the truth and the light because of the dark, but I never lost love for myself and everyone else. I might have shut myself off to the family that I have and to the world around me, but I never lost sight of love.

Back to the battery and screw, they seemed to be good friends because fighting did not break out. Then one night, I began to go around my room checking on all my friends and toys. When I got to my battery and screw, I took my knife and went to touch the battery. It started attacking my knife like it was jealous with a vengeance. I could hear the chopping sounds of metal to metal. I mean, I *knew* that there would be places in my knife that had been damaged by the attack.

My attention was drawn to the screw, wondering what it might do if I placed the knife beside it. Well, it was not what I expected. I hovered the knife close to the screw. Right as I got up on it (maybe a little under an inch), the screw came up off the floor and attached itself to the knife. I did it again and again, just amazed at what I was witnessing. Boy, let me tell you all that, by this time, I called my room "the freak show," and let me tell you that *it was* a freak show! Finding answers didn't really matter to me at this point; I just wanted to know what I could find next. I was having fun, was I not? This drug, this addiction, had me so blind, lost in total darkness.

One day, this one buddy of mine came over and brought his so-called uncle, Bobby. He was left sitting in the den by himself, not knowing anyone. I asked Bobby if he would like to come to my bedroom so I could show him the freak show. Boy, did I ever get a look from him! He took that the wrong way. I explained that no, I didn't mean anything like *that*; it's just that my room was a circus. When we went in there, he was amazed by everything that was going on. He, like everyone else, asked how I was doing all that. My answer was, "I'm not. You tell me!"

We got down on the floor looking at everything, and I showed Bobby the battery. Let me tell you, he saw what I saw, and he heard what I was hearing. Then he asked, "What does the screw do?" I explained to him that the screw loved the knife and would attach itself to it. Then I handed him the knife, and when he got close to the screw, it came up off the carpet. When it attached itself to the knife, he kind of jerked. Boy, of all things, that screw did something to his brain because he could not quit! Bobby said that the knife or the screw had to be magnetic. So I began to grab whatever metal objects were around, but the screw would attach itself only to the knife.

Then, suddenly, he asked, "Where did it go?"

"What do you mean?"

"It disappeared in the carpet."

"You aggravated it to where it left," I explained.

He left my room, and I could hear him mumbling as he walked away. Shortly after that, I went back into the den, and Bobby was sitting in one of the kitchen chairs saying over and over, "There is no way that this is going on. No way that the screw would attach itself to the knife!" I asked him if he was okay, and he questioned, "That screw and knife—how did that happen?"

By this time, I was getting worried about him because he kept saying it over and over. Finally, his so-called nephew came back into the den. I told him what happened, and they went home. I called the next day and asked the nephew about Bobby, and he said, "My uncle finally quit talking about the screw and knife." I asked to talk to him, and when he got on the phone, I checked to see if he was okay. He reassured me that he was fine and had not had any dope for four or five days (so he said).

One day, Jeremy had a couple of his friends come over, Josh and Jeff. He wasn't home, so they hung around and waited. I had met these two guys a couple of times and thought they were pretty cool. This time, they had a couple of females with them named Tiffany and Mary. I thought that maybe it would be a good time to show them a magic trick with aluminum foil. I went to my room, got some pieces of foil that I knew would work, and took them into the den. "Watch," I said.

When I dropped a piece of foil, Mary spoke up, "I saw you drop it—where did it go?"

"Watch very carefully."

She could not understand. Amazed but yet puzzled, she asked, "Where did it go?"

I took the rest of what I had and, again, said, "Watch very carefully." Then I dropped all the pieces of foil.

The word to explain the look on her face was *baffled*. "Where did it go? I saw you drop it!"

I started explaining to her how it would hide from me in the den, but in my bedroom, I could play with it. Then I asked the question that I *loved* to ask people who had never been to my room before: "Would you like to come see my room?"

Let me tell you that she did not take that question the right way at all! "No, nothing like *that*," I explained. "I just wanted to show you the aluminum foil people."

So Mary came to my room and, just like everyone else, was amazed at what was going on. She tried to get Tiffany to come see, but she was gone out of her head.

Well, Jeremy never showed up, but Mary got my number and said, "You're pretty cool. I'll call you sometime."

I was thinking to myself that she really was not that pretty. To me, looks do help, but it's all about the heart, and I realized I had met someone that might really be a friend. Well, to make a long story short, I never heard from her and can say with all confidence that I never will.

CHAPTER 16

All during this time, it would sometimes happen that I would be in my room and start to see flashing lights. When I'd see them and take off to find out what was going on, there was never anybody there.

I was starting to get paranoid that someone was outside taking pictures. So I closed the blinds in my room, but eventually, the flashing lights reappeared. I stood there, watching the TV—nothing. So I thought that I would just turn off the TV, and let me tell you, the flashing lights eventually came back. Well, I accepted what was going on, seeing the lights but not acting on them.

Then, Jeff and Josh came over. We were all in the den when I saw flashing lights.

"Did you all see that?"

They replied, "See what?"

"Those flashing lights."

Of course, they did not see them.

Then, we were going down the hall talking, and there were the flashing lights again. This time, I didn't say anything.

"I saw it!" Josh called out.

"Saw what?" I asked.

"I saw the flashing lights," he declared. "It was like someone taking pictures!"

Later on that night, I came out of my room, and the two of them were creeping around in the house with their guns in their hands.

"What are you all doing?" I demanded. "Put those guns up."

They were like, "We hear someone."

It took a couple of seconds, but they put their guns away.

Not only would things happen before my eyes, but they would happen before my ears too. One night, I was in my bathroom doing whatever, and I could hear people talking about me. The reason I knew that was because every now and then, I could hear them say my name. So I concentrated on listening, and still, all I could hear was my name.

Okay, I'd had enough. I wanted to know who was talking and what they were saying about me. When I got in there, there was *nobody*. How could that be? I was listening to them, and I was hearing my name as plain as day.

A few times at night, I would hear people talking outside, so I would go out the front door and walk around the house, trying to figure out who it was. There were even times I could hear them moving around outside, right below the window. I would storm out the back door, trying to catch them.

I finally got sick and tired of it, so I closed the curtains. During the day, I cracked the window open just enough so it wouldn't be noticed. It got to the point where I would listen, not really being able to make out what was being said. This one time, though, I could hear them say, "Is he crazy or what?"

* * * * *

By this time, Sharon was coming over to the house to get dope for her and Dwayne who was now her new boyfriend. I didn't allow that, so when I would find out she'd been there, I would come unglued. I'd heard from a few people that she and Dwayne lived in a garage about the size of my bedroom with a mattress on the ground. Their electrical power came from an extension cord running from the neighbor's house, and there was no running water.

One day, the two of them came to the house while I was there. Dwayne stayed in the car while Sharon came to talk to me. She explained that they were going to the beach to meet her mom, and she needed a shower because she hadn't had one for four or five days. She actually tried to sweet-talk me into using the shower at my place.

"Are you joking me?" I snapped. "*No!*"

Then came the bribery. "We were going to pay you," she bargained. "We can pay you now or after we get done."

Let's think about this: I am a drug addict, and I have a chance to get free drugs. Well, the answer was still *no!*

I had once had so much love for Sharon, and sometimes, I would wonder why she could leave what she had with me. I live in a nice home, and she had given all that up to live in a garage. Not just the living situation, but I had seen how they fought like cats and dogs. Answer number one—Dwayne had a car, so she could support her drug habit. Welcome to the meth/ice world!

If I knew then what I know now, I would have run as fast as I could and not look back. But this just goes to show—live and learn. Love is blind, and, boy, was I ever blind beyond recognition. Time may have passed, but even now, I would like to know that Sharon is okay. There will always be a special place in my heart for her. Maybe she'll even read this book. To her and anyone else I may have crossed paths with, good luck, and I hope and pray that you'll find the light and the truth because where that is, love is never-ending. True love, unconditional, that lasts forever!

CHAPTER 17

The things that happened during this time were unbelievable but not because I witnessed them and survived the nightmare. Again everything that I have told you is God's honest truth. This nightmare was one I lived by choice because *I am an addict.* The one saying that I can say that I *hate* is: "Once an addict, always an addict." Thinking of that saying is a nightmare in itself, but it's something that I can look back on. I will not say, "I will never use again," because every time I say *never,* never sneaks up on me and bites me in the butt. So I'm here to say that I am fully committed to staying sober, knowing that I have the light if I ever need it—for the Light is the only way to truth and lots of love.

* * * * *

Okay, we've come to the part of my story where I started to get answers to all of my questions. It took me living this nightmare to find these answers, which I will share with you. Things are fixing to change for the better, so hold on, and I promise that I will give you the answers that took me through this nightmare.

One afternoon, the horrible, disgusting smell seemed to come early. We had company over, so I picked up one of the little figurines and took it into the den to show the girl who was visiting. I thought this particular figurine looked pretty cool at the time, so when I showed it to the girl, she asked, "What's that?" After taking a closer look, she commented, "Cool, how did you make it?"

"The devil gives them to me."

She looked at me like usual. "No, he didn't."

I was like, "Then you tell me how they just appear."

Let me tell you, it is fixing to get crazy.

Later that night, Karen and I were left home all alone. I was in the room she shared with Jeremy when we heard three slamming sounds. She kind of got startled and whispered, "Did you hear that?"

When she asked that, let me tell you that the thoughts running through my head were incredible. I looked at her and replied, "Yes I did, but I thought that you all told me I was crazy, yet you hear this also?"

"What is it?"

"It's the crawl space door under the house."

"Don't you need to go see what's going on?"

"*I know what it is!*" I exclaimed. "It's the devil, and he loves it under the house. It's one of his favorite places. He loves to go down there and make all kinds of noises."

Suddenly, we heard two car doors slamming outside. We looked at each other, and I stated, "They're here."

We looked out the window and couldn't see, so we went to the front door where I looked out the peephole. There was no car outside, and I told her so. She was in disbelief. Going back to the window, she insisted, "But I heard the car doors."

"I told you that the devil is here, and he is having fun with us."

We started walking away when we heard two car doors again. We looked at each other and went to check, but ditto—it was nothing. Once again, we started to walk away when I heard someone in my ear say, "*Boo!*"

"Did you hear that?" Of course, she didn't, so I explained, "They're really here—at the front door. I heard Jeremy's voice." So I looked out the peephole, and she went to the window.

"I don't see his car," she told me. I started down the hall without her; then she exclaimed, "There is something in the closet!"

When she said those words, I got scared. I mean, I was ready to bolt down the hallway. "Do not open that door!"

Something had to have told her to look in the closet, or she must have heard something, but I will probably never know. "But what if there's someone in there?" The closet door was already cracked, so she edged it open with her foot. Nothing.

We started back down the hall when we heard this commotion going on in the garage. It sounded like someone was running around, knocking things off the shelves. "What is that?" she pleaded.

"They're in the garage playing with us," I reasoned. So we ran to the garage door, turned the light on, and there was nobody!

We looked at each other and said, "But I heard the noises in the garage!"

I'm not sure what we talked about after that, but for some reason, from that time on, we never discussed what happened that night.

* * * * *

Time went on, and again, the horrible, disgusting smell came early. It had started that evening and stayed all night till morning. I went to Karen and Jeremy's room where Karen was by herself. I announced to her that the devil was there at the house.

That morning, something told me to look, and how I knew where to look, I have no idea. There on my nightstand where I had some of the foil boxes that I had made, I saw something that caught my eye. When I walked over to it, there was this pin that I had lost—a pin with a snake wound around it. I took it into Karen's room and showed it to her. She asked me where I got it, and I told her that the devil was there.

I went back into my room, and shortly after that, I started finding "gifts" everywhere. The gifts were people, demons, dogs, birds, and monsters that I'm sure were demons. The gifts were getting ridiculous to the point where I would sit down on the side of my bed, turn around, and there would be more that had appeared.

I started to believe that I was looking over the same ones, so I started tossing them against the wall. Well, that did not work because just as soon as I would turn around, there would be a new one. I really started getting scared because it would not stop.

I went back to Karen's room and told her that I was afraid.

"Why?" she responded.

"He won't stop!"

Shortly after, that we had company—a man and a young girl. I could overhear them talking, and I heard Karen say that I had told her that I was scared. They just kind of laughed about it. Eventually, both dealers, Del and Jeremy, arrived, and we all did our thing.

By this time, the smell was gone, but then things *got intense.* There were three big thumps at the front door. When I heard that, I knew who it was. Confirmation came when a voice shouted, "*Police!* Open up, or we're knocking the door down!"

Karen came running into my room exclaiming, "The police are here!" I started throwing stuff under my bed (like that was going to do any good).

Then again, a voice at the front door shouted, "Open the door, or we're coming in!"

No sooner had those words come out of their mouths when there were some serious thumping sounds. I knew exactly what that meant—entrance made.

All the hollering was going on. "Everyone down, now!"

I am telling you, what a rush. Drugs have nothing on these feelings. These are the feelings of reality—time to face the consequences.

I ran to my closet and threw blankets and clothes over myself, thinking that I was going to hide. I heard one of the policemen say, "There's a couple of them missing. Bring the dog in!"

The thought ran through my head, *What am I thinking? The dog will find me, and I will get chewed on, and that is something I am for sure that I do not want!* So I went to my bedroom door and stuck my hands out to show that I had no weapons.

The reality was back when they called out, "Come out with your hands up and get down on the floor with your hands behind your back!"

As I complied, one of them put their foot on my back, and my destination was certain when I heard the handcuffs. They took us outside, and, boy, what an audience there was—neighbors watching and all kinds of people driving by. It was crazy.

I finally got booked and spent nine days in classification. Then I got a little freedom and went to an open pod. You see, I have only been to jail one time other than this, and it was a horrifying experience. So when I got to my bunk, I was nervous—scared to death—even though I accepted what I had done to myself.

I made friends pretty fast, not seeing the motive. My dad always used to tell me, "Learn to read people." Still, they earned my trust, not knowing everything coming out of their mouths was a lie. My lesson to learn was that you *cannot*—at least I can't—read people in jail. They will get you blinded and take everything you have. Thankfully, I got moved to another pod, and that was where everything changed.

CHAPTER 18

I liked the new jail pod better because we did not have as much freedom. The cellmate that I had, Jack, was pretty cool; he just would not take a shower. So almost every day, I would clean the cell because of the smell. Then Jack got moved, and I made a request to room with this guy, Randy, that I met in classifying. He had even dated Sharon at one time.

We had quite a bit in common, including the girlfriend, so we talked about her and her infamous attitude. Before long, though, we started talking about GOD. It seemed that Randy could answer every question that I asked, and to the best of my knowledge, it sounded correct. By the time he got out, I was reading the Bible, and when he left, he gave me his Bible.

Randy had gotten his Bible while he was in there; what we call a "prison Bible." He told me that when he was attending church in jail once, the preacher had said, "I'm going to leave this Bible here, so if anybody wants it, please take it." He told me that as soon as the preacher laid it down, he went straight to it and picked it up. So after Randy left, I started reading more and more.

Then, the most amazing day of my life happened. Boy, let me tell you that *I would not trade this day for the world!* I was standing by the phone, fellow inmates everywhere, when this Voice said, "*Do you know why you are here?*"

Why would I think that? How stupid, I know why I'm here. Then I realized, *Hey, that was not my voice.* I looked up and asked, "God, was that You?"

Well, I didn't get an answer, so I continued, "I've been doing wrong. I've been doing drugs!"

Then, He spoke again and said, *"No, I want you back."*

Let me tell you that my thoughts were beyond I do not know. I went back to my cell, opening my Bible, thinking, *Oh my god! God just talked to me!*

From that day on, life has never been the same. When I walked out of the cell, it was like being on a cloud, like I was in a dream.

I got a new cellmate named Brad, and he was pretty cool; really could not ask for a better one. We talked sometimes, but we read the Bible, and I would ask him questions. I was confident that everything he said was accurate.

One morning, I woke up, and Brad was getting ready. I thought that it was breakfast, but he was actually getting ready for prison. So he unpacked his stuff and left me a radio, lotion, and a brand-new deodorant. As he was walking away, I heard someone hollering at him, but he did not turn around.

Later that morning, when we finally got outside, this big guy, Holden, came up to me and asked what I was going to do with all the stuff that Brad had left behind. I told him that I was planning on keeping it to use because I didn't know how long I was going to be in there. Holden said that he would make sure that I got a couple of extra food trays if I were to give him the deodorant and some of the lotion. So I made the deal with him, saying, "Don't worry, I got you."

After a couple of days when we were in the lunch line, it was my turn, and I reminded him, "You haven't forgotten me?" I wish that I had kept my mouth shut because, boy, did he get mad and really raised his voice. As I was walking away, I thought, *That is it! I won't say anything again.*

Then, one day, I noticed that Holden was having problems and not getting his way. The one thing that drew my attention was the way he was acting. He didn't have a brown bag, which would have had food in it to trade for what he wanted. I began to laugh.

"Stop laughing!" When I heard that, I literally ducked because it sounded as if the voice was directly above me.

I looked up and questioned, "God, was that You?"

I got no answer. I looked out the window at Holden, and something came across my mind. Out loud, I stated, "An eye for an eye, and a tooth for a tooth. God, did You do this for me?"

Of course, no answer, but I've always heard of karma, and let me tell you, leave it alone! God will, on His terms, take care of things if He sees fit, but you have got to turn the other cheek. Let me tell you, easier said than done.

* * * * *

The time came for me to go to court. I couldn't sleep, so I stayed up all night reading the Bible and writing. As I read, I kept getting these messages that were kind of confusing. I didn't know what to do with that, but I reminded myself to trust God.

Court time came, and I was put in the bullpen, a place where they keep prisoners until it is time for them to appear. People were asking me about my charges, and they were telling me that I was going home. (Even the day before, people had been telling me that.)

I asked every one of them, "How do you know?"

Each one said almost the same thing, "Trust me, you are going home today."

So I marched through court, got my bail lowered, was ordered to rehab, and was released. I had spent thirty-eight days in jail, and now I was going home. When they called my name, people were coming up to me saying they had never seen anyone get out so fast after court.

When I walked outside, I felt freedom, and let me tell you, all that freedom feels so great. I got one night with my parents before I went off to rehab. I ate and drank, ate and drank, and ate and drank even more. I ended up not sleeping from drinking so much coffee. The next morning, Dad fixed me a breakfast fit for a king: fried eggs, peppered bacon, toast with butter, tomatoes, and of course, coffee! Then I started on a honey bun.

At the scheduled time, I caught the van that picked up clients for treatment, and I was on my way. The ride lasted about four hours, and let me tell you, it was not so bad because I was free. I had made my mind up that I *wanted help* and that I was going to make this work.

I was admitted to Buffalo Valley on September 23, 2015. When we first got there, all the questions that I had to answer drove me crazy. The meal that I ate in between was awesome, though, and by this time, I was really feeling the love.

I could tell that they really cared because the staff seemed genuinely concerned about me. By the time they took me down to where I would be staying, I was acting like myself, playing around and joking with everyone.

I had a few minutes to myself, so I found the vending machine and got some snacks and a drink. The next thing I knew, a young man came up to me. He introduced himself as Mike, and we started talking.

"What's your DOC?" he asked. I didn't know what he meant, so he explained, "Your drug of choice." I told him that it was ice/meth; his was pills.

Another young man named Aaron came up and started chatting. Turned out his drug of choice was the same as mine. As we talked, I began to realize that I really felt a connection with them. We started discussing what to expect and what time we were supposed to be in bed.

Before I knew it, it was bedtime, and I thought to myself that it would be so cool to have these two guys as roommates. As I walked toward my room, I was kind of nervous, but when I opened the door, boy, was I surprised to see Mike and Aaron there! What a great way for God to remind me that He had already arranged everything.

CHAPTER 19

I was beginning to get settled in, but there was something serious that kept burning in my mind. You see, my mother had cancer, and her first chemo treatment was on a Tuesday. I remembered it that Wednesday night. Well, that was not a good time to remember because the counselors could not give me phone privileges. Still, I thought that I just had to try.

I went up and explained my situation, and I heard one of them say to the other, "Try to get ahold of a supervisor." I walked away thinking, *Patience. God always says, "Be patient."*

Well, it was not looking good because Friday came, and I was gone out of my head—I mean, spun out—thinking nothing positive; everything was negative. I haven't mentioned it before, but I am bipolar (manic depressive), so in my head, I was ready to explode any minute.

It was during that time that we were given a form to fill out. I only saw that particular form one time in twenty-eight days, but it was a questionnaire about how we felt. Let me tell you that when I filled that paper out, I shared exactly how I was feeling, no sugar added!

The class was dismissed, and I was walking around the building, praying. Then Amanda, my counselor, came over the intercom and asked me to please come to her office. When I got there, I didn't even get the door closed, and she looked at me puzzled, very concerned. "Mr. Moore," she began, "we've looked over your form, and this is not the Mr. Moore that we know. This is actually kind of disturbing."

She asked me what the problem was, so I explained about my mother and how I really needed to talk to her.

This turned out to be a great thing. Amanda changed my code color from *red*, which meant no privileges, to *yellow*, and that meant one phone call as long as I got ahold of someone. So that evening around 6:00 or 7:00 p.m., I called and got the answering machine twice. I looked at my phone card, reminding myself, "It will be okay, I'll call her tomorrow."

So the next day, around 1:00 or 2:00 p.m., I called the house and got the answering machine. Again. Then I called my mom's phone and got the answering machine. I called my dad's and—answering machine. I called my sister and then my niece, and both times, I got an answering machine. Instantly, I was out of my head, thinking negatively, terrified that something was wrong. I was convinced that nobody was answering their phones so that they wouldn't have to tell me bad news because of the shape that I was in. I just knew that my mother was in the hospital, having complications with chemo, maybe even dying.

Let me tell you, mental illness is *no joke*. If you happen to know someone like this who just goes off to be alone, it is very dangerous. At this point, suicide seems to be the only way out, so be careful with us.

By this point, I was spun the freak out, beyond baffled. *Gone.* So I mumbled a few things and gave the phone back to the office staff. The whole time, they were saying, "Calm down, it will be okay."

I went to my room, crying like a baby, praying to our Father in heaven, asking Him for help because I was so torn up over my mom. As I prayed, my head turned, and I looked directly at my Bible. I grabbed it, knowing exactly where I was going. I ran out the front door, passed everyone going down the hill, not caring if I was going out of boundaries. Right now, I had one thing on my mind, and that was to pray, trying to fix this.

At the bottom of the hill, there was a little picnic table where I could be all alone to pray and read my Bible. So I began praying, "Please help me, Father. Please help! I need to know about my mother. Please let me know!"

Then, I heard, "They're at the lake."

That's stupid! I told myself. *Why would I think that? Mom just had her first chemo, and she probably doesn't feel good.*

The voice continued, "And they have your children."

Let me tell you, *that* I thought was ridiculous. It just didn't make sense. There was no way that my parents would be at the lake with my children because my mom wouldn't be feeling well enough to take care of them.

Then, I noticed that my depression was lifting; that was something I couldn't do on my own. Usually, when my depression hits, it seems that no one cares or that they think that I'm crazy. In my case, though, it's kind of easy to cure—all it takes is getting a hug and knowing that someone really cares.

Then, it hit me. *He* cared. I looked up and said, "God, was that You?"

Well, I didn't get an answer, so I thought I would read my Bible since I had planned on it. While reading, I highlighted things that I wanted to remember; things that I thought He was trying to tell me. My Bible read:

> I have not been speaking to you plainly. But
> a time is coming when I will speak clearly. Then I
> will tell you plainly about my Father. When that
> day comes, you will ask for things in my name. I
> am not saying I will ask the Father instead of you
> asking him. (John 16:25–26 NIRV)

Let me tell you that my mind was scrambling. *Oh my god!* I thought. *That was really Him, and He is still talking to me through the Bible!* So I closed my Bible. *This is crazy—thinking that GOD just spoke to me!* Again, *No way!*

When I went back up, I never said anything to anyone. I was just the same old person before all this happened. It was about 5:00 or 6:00 p.m., so I called my parents' house phone and got the answering machine right off the bat. Then I tried my dad's phone, and someone picked up, but it immediately disconnected, so I called back.

That time, my mom answered. "*Mom!*" I blurted. "Mom, how are you doing? Are you okay?"

"I'm doing fine!"

"Really, Mom? You're okay?"

"I'm fine!" she repeated. "Guess where we're at?"

Let me tell you, when she said that, the thoughts that I had were, *I know—I know where you are!* Still, I had to ask, "Where? Where are you?"

"We're at the lake," she stated.

"Really, Mom—really, you're at the lake?"

"Yes," she confirmed, "and guess who we have with us!"

When she said that, I felt so much joy thinking, *I know, I know!* "Who, Mom? Who do you have with you?"

"We have your babies with us, do you want to talk to them?"

I can't believe this, I was thinking. *It's true that GOD told me all this!*

I talked to all of my babies, talked to my dad, and talked to my mom. *It was a miracle!* I will remember that day for the rest of my life.

If I could have done anything differently on the phone that day when my mom said, "Guess where we are," I would have told her, "You're at the lake, and you have my children!" I've asked myself a bunch of times why I didn't do that, and just a week ago, I realized that the reason I never did it is that the book that God wrote is already written. Me giving the answers to my mom evidently was not written in His book; therefore, I did not say anything. So I will just go with these quotes: "It is what it is," "Everything happens for a reason," and, "Accidents just do not happen. They are caused!"

CHAPTER 20

By then, I realized that the things that were going on were of God, so I began to pray even more. Then I came up with this brilliant idea. I was always running out of creamer and sweetener for my coffee (I had kind of drifted away from sugar because it took more of it to sweeten stuff). You see, at rehab, we were limited on the amount of coffee we could drink. As long as we were eating, we could drink it, but after going outside, we couldn't come back in for refills.

The one thing I noticed about addicts (myself included) was that coffee seemed to be a serious *want*. I think it's because of the energy in the caffeine. Most of us didn't have the money or time to get coffee. Condiments, including sugar and creamer, were big things that we were always running out of. The thing was that there was this woman who worked in the cafeteria who was good at catching people, so trying to re-up was dangerous. It's not that we'd really get into trouble, but she would make a scene.

Anyway, I began walking around, talking to our Father in heaven, asking Him for help. "I put it in Your hands," I prayed. In a way, I felt as if this was wrong, but still, I put it in His hands. "It's up to You if You see fit for me to have more coffee, but if not, then I will accept it as it is."

Well, the next meal that we had was amazing. As people were finishing up, they would walk by dropping their sugar, sweetener, and creamers on my table. Some even asked, "Do you want these?" From that day on, I never had problems running out of condiments—just so long as we didn't get caught!

This led me to think that I needed to put God first, so I began walking around the building talking to Him. "How do I know to put You first? Because I *want* to put You first." I further explained to Him, "I know You're up there. I just don't understand how I will know stuff—it's like I see my children and my family, but I still don't understand how I will know."

I kept on wondering, "*How?* How will I know?" thinking that He was going to tell me. I mean, why not? He had spoken to me before. Then it happened; I realized that I had quit praying, but that was crazy. I did not remember stopping, so I asked God, "Was that Your answer—making me stop praying?"

As I said that, an incredible feeling came over me. It was like no other. It seemed to almost take my breath, and as I exhaled, it was like a relief. Then I looked up and declared, "God, You actually touched me. *You* actually touched *me!*"

To this day, I really can't explain the feeling, but it was like seeing your children being born. Maybe another way to describe it is like when you are in love (new love), and you've been waiting all day to see your love. Then you see them, and that feeling of beauty that overcomes you is the best way that I know to explain what I call being touched by God. Remember that I was just *describing* the feeling because there is no way to put it into words.

* * * * *

During this whole time, I had a thing for writing pens. If I found a pen, I would keep it. Of course, if I found a pen and could figure out who it belonged to, I would return it. I don't understand why, but I really liked pens. So I was walking around the building, talking and praying to God, when something caught my eye. There was this pen; I mean, it was beautiful, a pinkish purple. I picked it up, looked heavenward, and said, "Thank You, Father!"

When I took a couple of steps, I heard a voice tell me, "It's not yours—you know whose it is." Immediately, I understood. The clues were there. Though I didn't exactly know who the pen belonged to, for some reason, I turned around and looked. When I did that, I realized that the pen had been under the door of a vehicle. The thought struck me that the pen must have fallen out as the person was getting out of their vehicle. I reasoned that it must have belonged to them.

I walked around the vehicle, checking to see the make, model, and color. There was even a slogan on the back of it. I was on a mission, going straight into the building and to my counselor's office to find out whose pen it was. When I got there, I asked Amanda who the vehicle belonged to, and she wanted to know why. "I found this pen under the door, and God told me that it wasn't mine," I explained, "so I need to know whose vehicle that is."

Amanda was the only person that I had ever told that God spoke to me, and up to this point, this was the only time. She told me who the vehicle belonged to, but the location was downstairs in another wing, and I had no idea where that was. So I checked around and went to find the woman who owned the vehicle. When I arrived, I knocked and heard her murmur something. As I opened the door, she called out, "I'm with a client, and it might be a while."

I told her that I would be waiting outside when they were done. It was a hot day, and I was at the corner of the building against the block wall getting no breeze, just direct sunlight. I even began sweating a little bit. *Gee, it sure is hot,* I told myself. *I'll just wait here.*

After a while longer, I thought, *Man, it is really getting hot right here! Maybe I can come back.* Then I reasoned, *Well, if I leave, then I might not come back.* I considered it some more. *Well, I can come back. It is hot!*

I began to wonder, *Why am I waffling back and forth in my head over this? It's ridiculous!* Then I realized that this back-and-forth stuff was not me. It was the devil. Out loud, I announced, "I am not leaving, and I am giving this pen back!" The next thing I realized, I was literally at peace in my mind. The waffling had completely quit.

The client finally came outside. As they left, I came up with an idea. I took the pen and scribbled some of the colors on the palm of my hand because I really wanted that pen. When I finally made it to the woman's desk, I asked, "Did you lose something?"

She began to look around chuckling, "I'm sure I have. I'm always losing things."

When she looked up at me, the moment came, and I asked, "Is it this color?"

Immediately, she looked down at the nametag that she wore around her neck and exclaimed, "My pen!" I returned it to her, explaining how I had found it underneath her vehicle door and that it must have fallen out when she got out of the vehicle.

Returning an ink pen may not seem like a big deal to some people, but it was an important step for me—learning to discern our Father's voice and trusting Him enough to obey Him.

CHAPTER 21

One night during rehab, I had taken my medicine and was settling in for the evening. I was wanting some coffee, so I went and got a cup out of the vending machine, which was available at just about any time. I sat down with my cup of coffee and found myself talking to this guy. As we continued our conversation, I began to feel really sleepy. My medication usually makes me feel drowsy in about thirty to forty-five minutes. This time, though, I noticed that it seemed to hit me earlier than usual, like a ton of bricks.

I tried to listen to the guy, fighting to stay awake, but I was losing the battle. *Man,* I thought to myself, *I sure wish that he would hurry up so I can go to bed.* I didn't want to be rude and walk away, but I finally told him that I was very sleepy and needed to get to my room. As I got up, I felt very weak and disoriented. It was as if I was going to fall asleep walking—almost like I was drunk. *This is crazy!* I told myself because of the way I was feeling.

Going into the building, I was actually leaning against the wall to keep from falling because I was so weak. When I turned the corner, I thought that I had better go see the nurse because I felt like something bad was going to happen—like I wasn't going to make it.

I made it to the nurse's station and told her, "I think I need my blood pressure checked."

She took one look at me and ordered, "You need to sit down. What's going on?"

I started to tell her what had happened but got to where I couldn't hold my head up. "Stay with me!" she kept saying over and over. When she took my blood pressure, she announced, "It's 72/45. I'm going to check it manually—just stay with me!"

This time, my blood pressure read 42/70. "Stay with me," the nurse urged again. "I'm calling the EMT because something is wrong."

While waiting, I asked her about my blood pressure because I'm blind to how all that works. When she explained about the readings, she still continued to repeat, "Stay with me!"

Each time I would reply, "I'm trying, but it's hard to keep my head up, and it keeps getting dark!"

Finally, the EMTs showed up, and they took my blood pressure. It still wasn't good, so they got me in the ambulance and started hooking me up and starting an IV. The EMT kept reading this little paper, and I asked him, "What's the matter?"

"Not sure, let me get another reading." Then he looked at me and determined, "It seems to be your heart, but we won't know until we have more tests done at the hospital."

I admit I got a little alarmed, but when I noticed how bright it was in the ambulance, I felt like it was okay. Then I thought about my family and began to pray—actually talking to God as if He was right there! Then again, isn't God always there? Answer: *yes*, He's always there!

As I prayed, I told God that if He wanted me, then I was ready, but I also told Him that I would love to be here for my family and watch my children grow up. As I prayed, the EMTs and I decided to go to a hospital a little farther away. It was more up-to-date with heart technology, and if something was to go wrong, then they would not have to rush me there after the fact.

We got to the hospital, and it was test after test, but here's the thing—the tests all came back normal. I stayed overnight and was discharged the next day with a clean bill of health. The doctors just couldn't explain it. The episode I'd had the night before was a mystery to them.

To me, it wasn't so mysterious. I believe the enemy, Satan, was trying to keep me from following our Father's path and from sharing my story. He may have laid me low for a time, but we know that Jesus has the ultimate victory in the end!

CHAPTER 22

Back at Buffalo Valley, I was carrying my Bible most of the time unless I was out running. When I would go running, I would leave my Bible sitting on the couch thinking that just maybe someone would pick it up and start reading. So one day, I came in from a run, sat down, picked up my Bible, and heard a voice say, "Put your Bible up."

I began looking around to see what was going on because I thought that someone was getting upset, and I didn't want to cause any trouble, so I went and put it up.

A few days later, I put my Bible on the couch again, hoping that just maybe someone would get interested in it and read it. When I came back in from running and picked up my Bible, again, that voice said, "Put your Bible up." Just like the first time, I started looking around, not noticing anyone, but I went and put it up anyway. I was really confused, not understanding why the voice was telling me to do that.

Then, this man from a local church came in for Bible study, and for some reason, I had two days all by myself with him. Let me tell you that he could not talk for answering the questions that I had. Then again, isn't that what Bible study is all about? Eventually, I told him about the voice telling me to put the Bible up. He looked at me and asked, "Did you?"

"Yes," I admitted.

"Why did you do that?"

"I thought that God told me to because it was bothering someone."

Well, apparently, what I did was not the right thing to do because the man explained, "That voice was the devil because God would never tell you to put the Bible away."

After that, the voice never again told me to do that.

* * * * *

I was hanging out one day when I happened to hear someone talking about how they would like to have a calendar. When I heard that, it made me think that it would be nice to have one too to keep up with how many days I had left at rehab.

The next day, I was going to church for the first time since I'd been at rehab. We had to catch a bus on Sunday morning to get to the church. When I got on the bus, I went to the back and sat down. There, I noticed this little card about the size of a business card. I picked it up, and there was a picture on it: a blue sky with hills overlooking the ocean with the tide flowing onto the sand. There, written on the card was a saying in quotes: "*What is impossible with man is possible with God* (Luke 18:27)."

Huh, I thought. When I turned the card over, I was amazed at what I saw. There in my hands was a pocket calendar! *This is crazy!* Of course, I said thanks to our Father because I just never knew things could happen that way—but guess what—they do! My saying today is that knowing God and believing that all the Bible says is true: "With God, the sky's the limit!" Think of it this way: we have never found the limit in the sky and never will, so there are no limits to God.

The church the bus took us to was First Baptist Church of Hohenwald, Tennessee. I had been going there for about two weeks when this woman leaned over to me and said, "I want you to know that I pray for you all at the rehab center every day." Well, that was awesome! I felt very happy to hear her say that and began chatting with her.

The woman's name was Sue, and I remember talking to her about the shepherd. At the time, I really didn't understand the full meaning of the story, but today, I do, and it is still one of my favorites. So I kept telling her, "He makes me feel special."

In return, Sue would say, "Well, we're all special, no one is more special than the other."

"I know, but you don't understand," I would insist. "I feel as if He wants me to do something."

"He wants us all to do something."

Then again, I would say, "You don't understand."

When church was over, we walked to the door, and Sue asked, "Are you going to be back next week?"

"Of course."

She asked if she could sit with me, and I told her that I would love for her to.

I went to the front desk looking around for a pen and asked them if they had any. Well, they were out and said that they would try to have some the next week. As I was walking away, I realized that I had lost sight of Sue and wished that I could have seen her to tell her goodbye.

Just as I was going out the door of the church, I saw her, marching as if she was on a mission! Come to find out, her mission was to find me because she had a surprise—a pen! I gave her a hug, and we departed.

When I made my way onto the bus back to rehab, a couple of the guys said, "You made a friend!"

* * * * *

I was getting close to finishing rehab. Just a week left, and I'd be going home. We were still talking about God and having so much fun with everyone. When it was time to go to church, I walked in the door, and there was my friend, Sue, waiting on me. We greeted each other and asked how one another was doing.

"May I sit with you?" she requested.

"I would love for you to."

As the service was about to start, I mentioned what we had talked about before that I felt as if there was something special that God wanted me to do. She replied to me saying that God has something special that he wants us *all* to do. "You don't understand," I countered.

During all that time, I never revealed that God had spoken to me or all the prayers that He had answered (and answered really quick!) During the service, the preacher said something about telling the world about Jesus. Sue kind of nudged me with her elbow, and when I looked at her, she gave me a smile. I thought to myself that just maybe God led her to do that, and that was what I was looking for.

By the time church was over, my mind was wondering about what God saw in me personally. What did he have for me that I could possibly do? I didn't realize it at the time, but a couple of months later during this journey called life, He would give me that answer.

* * * * *

The time came for me to leave Buffalo Valley, but I wasn't going home on the van that brought me there. I was kind of worried about who was going to be taking me home. The waiting game began, and let me tell you that during that time, I had all kinds of different feelings. In a way, I really did not want to leave, but then again, I was excited about getting home to my family and beginning the new life that I really wanted to investigate.

So as I was waiting, a group session we called *gratitude* was going on, and that was one of my favorite meetings. I walked in and shared what I was grateful for. I explained to the group that it was up to them to decide to get sober and that no one could make them do it. I reminded them that once they were ready to walk the road to recovery, they should take it one day at a time.

We went on a break, and friends were coming up to me, telling me that they were going to miss me. I had other people coming up to talk about God. Some people told me about their experiences with drivers that took them to their destinations—that part was kind of bothering me since I still didn't know who was supposed to take me home.

The time finally came, and my ride showed up. After shaking hands, the first thing the driver noticed was the book in my hand— the Bible. Let me tell you, God was still taking care of me because he actually cared. The entire ride, the top discussion was about the Lord!

When I arrived home, it was late. As I was approaching the front door, I noticed that the front window was open, so I hollered out to Mom and Dad. I invited my new friend inside, and they asked him if he wanted something to eat because they were just starting to fix their plates. He said he needed to get home himself, so he had to decline.

After he left, we fixed ourselves a plate, and I actually got to eat some home cooking. I will say one thing about the food at rehab—it was excellent. I heard people complain, but let me say seriously, the place was awesome, and the food was awesome. (Of course, no matter where you go, someone will always complain about something.)

Once I settled in, I had to go back to court. I already had myself committed to an IOP program (intensive outpatient program). I was out before the judge even came into the courtroom. My lawyer took me out in the hall and told me that the district attorney had said that they were proud of me and to keep up the good work. My next court date was scheduled, and that was that.

I have since graduated from IOP and, to this day, still go almost every time there is a meeting. Hearing people talk about their life struggles and overcoming addictions really helps. To tell you the truth, sometimes, I get more out of it today than when I desperately needed it. In other words, I'm still learning. To me, the healing and help that I've gotten from coping skills are tools I continue to use today. As it stands now, I'm still on probation for my actions. I'm not really worried, though, because I know who has my back.

CHAPTER 23

After class one day, I walked up to my teacher and announced, "I'm going to write a book!"

"What about?" he asked.

"I'm not sure," I told him, "but it's going to be crazy!"

Then, my preacher, Brother Tony, brought me home, and I shared my book idea with him. The conversation was pretty much the same. A week or so passed when I had an idea what I was going to write about, but I'm not a writer.

On another ride home, Brother Tony asked, "Have you started writing your book yet?"

"No."

"Why not?"

When I told him that I didn't know, he suggested that I keep a journal. Something simple, like a notepad to keep with me so as I remembered things, I could write them down and not forget.

The next morning, I woke up, and dates were just running around in circles in my head. I was trying to figure out what they were, so I went downstairs to the kitchen to see if I could write them down. (It turns out the dates were important days in my journey: my arrest, going to rehab, and coming home.) As I got downstairs, didn't really have to look, there was a notepad and a pencil, like just waiting for me. As soon as I picked them up, let me tell you, I began hearing voices in my head. The voices were not happy; they were scaring me. They never threatened me; they were just telling me to stop writing. "What did we tell you? I mean it, stop."

I was tripping out. This was crazy! I felt seriously scared. When I quit writing and walked away from the kitchen table, the voices completely ceased. I mean, it was just like pushing a button, and the voices were gone.

Another voice told me, "Pray about it."

"Father, I don't understand," I prayed. "If it is You, then I won't write this book. I know it may be bad in the beginning, but it all comes back to You. People need to know the truth. Please let me know!"

Before I could get out of the kitchen, I heard, "Go back and write." I picked up my pencil and opened the notepad to begin writing again. As I worked, I realized there were no more voices!

I can say one thing about our Father, the only God—when you expect something like an answer, forget it. He works on His terms and His terms only. Trust me, quit looking for an answer because when you do, all is forgotten—*bam*—there it will be. I'm not saying that He doesn't answer prayers fast, it's just that you need to remember that you're dealing with all capabilities with Him; that's why He is God, our Father!

* * * * *

My life was back on track and going great when I remembered the critters (demons) that I had in my house. I began to talk to my preacher about getting rid of them, and I thought that I could cast them out.

One day, I got my dad to take me by my house to pick up a pair of shoes that I had there. While I was at it, I thought I would show the critters who was boss. I took my Bible into my house, got my shoes, and raised my Bible up, saying what I thought was appropriate. Let me tell you that by the time I walked out of my house, the feeling that I had was unexplainable—emptiness, but at the same time, there was confusion in it, maybe a little fear. By the time I sat down in my dad's truck, I was looking at my house, thinking, *What just happened?* This feeling was taking over me. I felt as if I was in shock because it was nothing I had ever felt before.

When I went back to church, I told Brother Tony what I had done. I tried to describe the feeling and asked him, "What went wrong?"

"*Faith*," he revealed. "Your faith isn't strong enough."

A short time after that, me and the preacher's wife, Sister Flo, were talking. I was sharing the story about the glitter bugs and told her that my house was full of demons. She finally looked at her husband and said, "Tony, do you want to go see what he's talking about?"

Boy, I was getting excited, thinking, *It is fixing to go down!*

Brother Tony finally agreed, "Sure, we can go by there."

Sister Flo arranged for her sister, Rachel, to come with us. When we got to my house, I warned them. As soon as Rachel walked into the house, she commented, "Used to, when we walked in this house, you could feel the love, but now it feels empty. Nothing."

I took them to my room and showed them under my bed. They never really said anything, but they did see something. Like the dealers had told me, "When the dope is gone, then things will go back to normal."

Well, I will say one thing—things changed somewhat, but they did not go back to normal.

Normal. My definition of *normal* that I have sought out for many years would be nonexistence and a figment of the imagination. Another one I heard the other day is, "The definition of normal is the setting on your dryer."

Anyway, Tony kind of looked around, and then it started. Flo spoke up, "Let's hold hands."

Brother Tony raised his Bible and called down our Father, Jesus Christ, and the Holy Spirit, asking them to take care of the problem that existed in that room. Then we went into the next room, and again he asked the Lord to cleanse the room and under the house. When we went into the next room, I could feel something different, but he called them down once again, and they took care of business! It came time for the den and where it was open to the kitchen, and again raising his Bible, he asked the Lord to cleanse the room.

When we went to the last bedroom, it happened. Even before Tony said a word, I asked, "Does it seem colder in here?" I had no sooner spoken when, let me tell you, what we experienced was beyond baffling! It felt as if the aluminum spiders had come back to life and were out for revenge. They were all over me in great numbers, biting me. It was driving me crazy, and I was trying to wipe them off.

You know, the preacher and I are great friends now, but I have never to this day asked him why it took him so long to call them down. At the same time, I don't know if he himself had ever witnessed what I call a brutal attack.

While this was going on, his wife was saying, "They can't hear you!"

"I know," I cried out, "but they're all over me!"

Then my ears heard something beautiful, and it was Brother Tony asking the Father, His Son Jesus Christ, and the Holy Spirit to come take care of that room and get rid of the evil. By the time he was done, I had started sweating and was standing up, holding hands with everyone else. Sister Flo was worn out, acknowledging that she was exhausted. Let me tell you that she herself was praying the whole time, not slacking one bit.

There was one more room to go—the garage. By this time, I was curious about what it held. I mean, seriously, I wasn't scared; I was just at a loss for words. So we went into the garage and held hands, and Tony raised his Bible and began praying, calling on God the Father, Jesus Christ, and the Holy Spirit.

Then it was clear. Nothing else happened.

I'd like to give my take on why things happened the way they did. Again this is speculation. When we held hands, Brother Tony began casting out the demons, and we went from room to room. They would leave because the Lord had shown them who the boss was! So when we got to that last bedroom, I'm guessing that the demons had gathered there thinking that Tony would forget that room. Then when they saw us coming, they attacked me before he started, trying to scare us off because they knew what was up. They had lost the battle, no longer allowed in my house. Thank you, Jesus, for loving us so much!

After we got done, and the demons had been evicted, Brother Tony asked if I had any oil to anoint the house. I found some vegetable oil and then second-guessed myself. *No, that's not good enough.* I was thinking olive oil because of reading the Bible, but the preacher assured me that it didn't matter what kind of oil.

Brother Tony put some oil on his finger and said a prayer. Then he spread it over the door entrance, using it as a barrier to keep the demons from returning. After that, he cautioned, "Never clean this off—it must always remain."

I took a permanent magic marker and wrote *God bless* on my wall. This is what I look at now as my conviction. To this day, when I walk into my house, the feeling is beautiful. You can feel the love once again!

CHAPTER 24

Time was carrying on, and I was doing a lot of walking. While I walked, I would pray and talk to God, asking a lot of questions. As I asked, He seemed to let me know the answers, and I really believe that the answers I came up with were the right ones.

Every time something happened, I wanted an answer. If the wind blew, I would try to figure out why. If the sun popped out from behind a cloud, or if a cloud covered the sun, I wanted an explanation.

One day, Dad needed to go to the store, and I went with him. While we were there, he requested, "Help me find—" (whatever item it was). When I started to look, though, I was in a panic. I just could not focus. I saw all the things on the shelves, and it was a task that I had never encountered. I began looking at all the people as they walked by and started worrying about them. I was burdened with the fear of them going to hell. As I passed by them, I would wonder, *Do they know Jesus? He is real, and I want them to know because I love them, and I want them to be safe.*

All I could think about was everyone else. I was scared to death, driving myself crazy over this. I walked home, and when I got there, I could hear a song playing on the radio that I loved. You see, I kept my radio on all the time—up so loud that when you came in the front door, you could hear it, and it was always on Christian music. Something came over me, and I went straight to my bedroom, got down on my knees by the radio, and prayed for help because I was so scared for everyone. I started crying and begging God for help. The way I saw the world and the people that were in it was driving me crazy.

So later that day (or the next), I realized that He had answered that prayer. I still loved people, but the fear had lifted. This gave me peace of mind, so I thanked God for that peace. After that, my eyes were opened to a new world. Anytime I had a problem, I could take it to God.

Even now, if He sees fit, so it shall be. The problem is, there is always a blindfold trying its darndest to block out the light. Still to this day, when something is not right, or I have a feeling that I don't like, I call upon the Lord. In His own way and His own time, He answers.

* * * * *

Following my time at rehab, I was still staying with my parents. Even though things had been cleansed at my house, unusual stuff would sometimes happen at theirs. The cats seemed to notice things the first few times I came into the house. They were so curious; they would walk around, smelling me as if something was different about me. I mean, literally, they were investigating me even though they knew me. Speculation: I've always heard animals see things that we don't. From what I've heard and seen, I believe it, especially with cats. Then again, think of it this way: cats are very curious, and as the saying goes, "Curiosity killed the cat."

This one time, my children came for the weekend. They fell asleep downstairs, so I went and got in bed. As I was lying there, I heard footsteps coming down the hall and thought that maybe one of Mom's cats was coming to visit me. Then I realized that the footsteps were too big, so I thought that one of my babies might be coming to sleep in my room with me. Then the footsteps grew quiet, and I blew it off.

It wasn't long before the footsteps started again. I watched the door, and when it opened, something came into the room and went under the bed. I thought, *Huh, what is that cat doing under the bed?* because I could hear it scuffling around under there. So I got up, turned on the light, and looked under the bed, but there was no cat. *But I heard it come down the hall, enter the bedroom, and go under the bed.* So I went to the next room to check things out, and nothing.

I lay back down, and instantly, fear took over. I *knew* what it was because I have played that game before. Faith rose up in me, and I resolved, *No! It does not work like that!* So I grabbed my Bible, with no doubt that what I was fixing to say was the truth. I raised it up, declaring, "God our Father, the Creator, Jesus Christ His Son, who was sent to be beaten and tortured so that we who believe and accept in our hearts, confessing our sins and giving it all to You, and the Holy Spirit who was sent from the Father—the same power that raised Jesus from the grave is in me, and I ask that You remove all evil from this room!"

After I did that, there was *no doubt* that what I asked for worked because I believed it then, and I still do.

* * * * *

Everywhere I went, God seemed to lead me to people who were searching for the truth. I had a friend that I had been talking to, and I explained what had been going on. He told me things that were going on with him. "I know what it is," he said, "and they don't like me talking to you."

My neighbor began to have problems at work. He looked at me and observed, "Since we have been having these discussions on the thugs (that is what he called the demons), work has not been going right. Things are happening that do not make sense, and I know what it is."

So one thing that I can tell you is, the more you share information exposing demons for what they really are, they will let you know—at least me and people I know.

In the meantime, I moved upstairs to my parents' house because this woman that I had talked to called and let me know that she wanted to publish my book. She said that she knows a lot of people who have had experiences like mine, but no one would write about it. "People need to know the truth," she told me, "and you can bring this issue to light. Maybe, just maybe, through this book, you can help open the eyes of people about what is going on."

I was upstairs in Dad's office when something in the hall kept catching my eye. Then I realized that the sun was out, coming through the window, but the hall was dark. I knew exactly what I was dealing with again, so at that very moment, I grabbed my Bible. I asked the Father, Son, and Holy Spirit to take care of the critters while I wrote. Then I asked, "Please, would You also cleanse the hallway so they can't bother me?"

Still, stuff was happening in my parents' house, and I knew what it was. I explained things to my parents and gave them all kinds of evidence as to the cause. My dad said, "They don't bother me," but I told them that I could take care of it.

It was then that I discovered a special way to pray, and to this day, I still pray this prayer: "Jesus, wrap Your robe around me because I need Your protection. I know as long as I am covered by You, nothing can happen to me." There's nothing magical about it and no trick to it because, with God, there's only *love*.

I started to wonder why stuff was happening the way it was. Then again, I was dealing with pure evil. I talked to Sue, the woman I had met at church during rehab, and asked her *why*. The answer she gave me, I know deep down in my heart, was right: "The demons don't want your book to be written because it's the truth, and they don't want people to know the truth." She went on to say, "Just think of the people that you will give answers to and the people that you could save by writing this book."

Now I know, and she knows, that I cannot save a life—only JESUS; but just maybe I can help open the eyes of someone to see the light, the truth, and plant a seed that blooms into the most beautiful flower—Jesus Christ!

Just being honest, I've always wondered why God let all this happen to me, but God *did not*. The problems were because of my decisions, and the answers to all these problems were there all the time. Even though I searched many times, I had to figure things out for myself. The devil is very tricky and, just being human, flesh and blood, has kept blinding me to the answer. Today, I know the answer, and even though I may be blindsided at times, the answer is and always will be *prayer*.

CHAPTER 25

Day by day, I kept learning more about our Father, Jesus His Son (our Savior), and the Holy Spirit. The lessons didn't always come the way I thought they would, though.

I got together with an old friend that had been clean for a while, except drinking. That made me want to drink, but I refused. We went to a movie together and decided to go again the next day. It was Sunday, but I thought it wouldn't matter to miss one day of church. But then, I missed that night and then Wednesday.

During that time, I found myself thinking that I could still have "fun." Even the people from IOP said that they liked this "new me." I seemed to be funnier. I had some of them over, and I even drank alcohol with them.

The next day, I felt disgusted by what I had done—*conviction*. I had been talking to this young woman, and she told me that I needed to quit beating myself up over it. So I recovered and started thinking differently, accepting things as they came.

Then I met a woman who was a little bit older than me. She came to my house, and we started drinking together. Reality hit—I was not the person that I wanted to be. I had a little talk with God and explained to Him that I wanted to be back where I had once been with Him.

Later on, the little things that used to happen kind of started then stopped. I explained to this woman the things that I had done. She looked at me and observed, "I don't think you want to be the person you found. I believe that you want that spiritual person back."

I replied, "The person that I found, I need to keep a hold of to a point, but I need the spiritual part of me back because of the things that would happen, and things that I would see."

I really loved being the person who carried on in my mind with God the Father, Jesus, and the Holy Spirit. Then I realized that didn't have to stop. Things today are great because God lets me know daily that He loves me. He even gives me little surprises every now and then, and I love it.

So I ask today, How much of God do you have? Do you just pray here and there? Do you carry Him around in your pocket and use Him when you need Him?

How many times a day do you tell Him that you love Him? How many times a day do you just thank Him for what He has done and is doing? No matter how many times you do these things, you can never, ever do these too much!

When you go to work, drive down the road or cook supper, let me tell you, put Jesus to work. No matter the job, if He is working with you, then what can go wrong? If you make a mistake, *you* made the mistake, but God let you make that mistake in order to give you knowledge. Next time, just so maybe you won't make it again, so thank Him for the knowledge.

One more question: How strong is your faith? Praying and talking to God is the best way to start and finish the day; but to make it even better, turn right around and rebuke Satan in the name of Jesus Christ. Tell him who is the king, and then tell him to get behind you.

* * * * *

Answers. The answers that I am about to share are God's honest truth, and I believe they are 100 percent correct. These answers came to me because the Lord gave me knowledge of the truth by letting me see for myself what is really going on in the world, angels and demons, principalities and powers—the spiritual realm.

I find myself talking to many people, asking what their DOC (drug of choice) is. Then I ask them, "Have you seen the shadow people?" Almost everyone has said yes! Then there are those who say, "No, but I see shadows."

Then I ask them, "Do you hear the voices?" Everyone who has seen demons also hears voices, so I tell them that what they have been hearing are the demons. "I bet that they try to get you to kill yourself, hurt someone, or do something bad."

They look at me and admit, "I thought that I was just hearing things or that my addiction was talking to me."

Then I reply, "No, that is them, and they are evil. That is why when they speak, it is all bad."

I did find one girl who told me, "I have a good voice *and* a bad voice."

After all the time we had talked, I never knew. She was very sick, an addict, and I remember that she used to be very suicidal. Still, I couldn't help but wonder, *Why two?*

The next time I saw her, I asked, "When you hear the good voice and the bad voice, what do they say?"

She explained, "They fuss back and forth, trying to convince me not to do bad things." So in my mind, when the voices start, they know that she is trying to give up, but the Lord wants to take her into His arms and show her the great love He has for her.

Now for more answers:

The smell—that horrible, disgusting smell was Satan himself. When that smell came, the house would come to life. Visually, it would change to a really light lime green, and things would come out of the wall that I could not even begin to explain.

The shadow people were demons because I would always see them outside at night. They were never in direct sunlight, but whenever they came out during the day, they would be in the house. Through the tricks they would do and the voices that I would hear, they would make themselves known. They would create problems, making people think that others were saying things about them or causing fights by making people think that someone did something to them. I was a witness to many problems that I knew were false.

All those times I was making love with my girlfriend when I saw other people—some I knew, some I didn't know—they were demons playing with us. They made us believe that we were having fun because, at the time, it seemed that way. Then again, we were blindfolded in the dark.

When I got this next answer reading the Bible, it hit me like a truck. The feeling that I got was almost like shock, and I know that God let me feel this way so that it would stick with me, and I could tell the world.

My Bible reads:

> Here is the judgment. Light has come into the world, but people loved darkness instead of light. They loved darkness because what they did was evil. Everyone who does evil deeds hates the light. They will not come into the light. They are afraid that what they do will be seen. But anyone who lives by the truth comes into the light. They live by the truth with God's help. (John 3:19–21 NIRV)

That also explained why when the sun was coming up, some of us felt disappointed that it was morning. We didn't want the dark to go away because we loved the dark—the dark was our friend. But now, I love the light. The light is the truth, and light represents Jesus Christ, my Savior.

Now to the insects. That time I looked under the bed, it scared me. I remember thinking, *What in the hell is that? Exactly*—it *was* that! There were so many insects, hundreds if not thousands of them. The floor was like looking under a fire, seeing the glow from all the coals, and the heat waves were like none I had ever felt. I did notice that the insects had long hair and that they kind of resembled a human except they had pointed ears. Their eyes were glowing a reddish hot pink, and they held something like a shield. There were also things that I would find, curled up as if they had tails.

I remember talking to the man who had come to do Bible study at rehab and told him that I thought that I had seen hell. He asked me what I had seen, and when I described the incident under the bed, he said from the way I told him and the look on my face that he believed that I had indeed seen hell. Looking back on it now, I believe it was "predestined"; that God allowed it, so Satan showed it, and I witnessed it so I could share it.

One day, as I was remembering the insects under the bed, something came to my mind. I thought that I had read something in the Bible. For some reason, I recalled Revelation and about where it was located. I didn't really know much about Revelation, so I began to look. It took a little bit, but when I found it, it was like going into shock. The feeling was sickening, and if someone had said something to me, I probably wouldn't have been able to speak. I wrote it down, but let me tell you, it was hard. I even dropped a few tears because I realized, *This is real!* I felt sorrow for the people that were not going to accept Christ as their Savior. Then the Lord spoke to me, and He took all the sorrow away.

> The fifth angel blew his trumpet. Then I saw a star that had fallen from the sky to the earth. The star was given the key to the tunnel leading down into a bottomless pit. The pit was called the Abyss. The star opened the Abyss. Then smoke rose up from it like the smoke from a huge furnace. The sun and sky were darkened by the smoke from the Abyss. Out of the smoke came locusts. They came down on the earth. They were given power like the power of scorpions of the earth. They were told not to harm the grass of the earth or any plant or tree. They were supposed to harm only the people without God's official seal on their foreheads. The locusts were not allowed to kill these people. But the locusts could hurt them over and over for five months. The pain the people suffered was like the sting of a scorpion when it strikes. In those days, people will look for a way to die but won't find it. They will want to die, but death will escape them.

> The locusts looked like horses ready for battle. On their heads they wore something like crowns of gold. Their faces looked like human faces. Their hair was like women's hair. Their teeth were like lions' teeth. Their chests were covered with something that looked like armor made out of iron. The sound of their wings was like the thundering of many horses and chariots rushing into battle. They had tails that could sting people like scorpions do. And in their tails they had power to hurt people over and over for five months. (Revelation 9:1–10 NIRV)

I believe the insects under the bed were the locusts in Revelation. I mean, all the details matched up to a T, exactly as it was described: down to the armor, the long hair, the crowns, and the human-like faces. The only two things that I did not see were their teeth and their wings; since they were looking at me, they never turned around. As for the noise that their wings made, like I said, they were looking at me, making no sounds—just waiting for the day that they might be able to do as they are told. You read it, so that day will come.

I continued reading Revelation, and as I got into it, I said a prayer and asked our Father to let me see more. Then later on that day, I went to my sister's house just as she was going to bed. Again I prayed, asking to see more. Then I fell asleep and woke up the next morning. My first thought was, *Well, I didn't see or dream about anything.* When I finally got back to Mom and Dad's, I started back reading. I prayed once again, *Let me see more.*

Then I got to Revelation 16—"The Seven Bowls of God's Anger."

> Then I heard a loud voice from the temple speaking to the seven angels. "Go," it said. "Pour out the seven bowls of God's great anger on the earth."
>
> The first angel went and poured out his bowl on the land. Ugly and painful sores broke

out on people. Those people had the mark of the beast and worshiped its statue.

The fourth angel poured out his bowl on the sun. The sun was allowed to burn people with fire. They were burned by the blazing heat. So they spoke evil things against the name of God, who controlled these plagues. But they refused to turn away from their sins. They did not give glory to God. (Revelation 16:1–2, 8–9)

Now I have read Revelation a few times and never saw it this way. After reading and praying, it was as if God let me know that I had seen this. The feeling was confusion, baffled for words like I was in shock from what I read. To me, this explained the sores that appeared on my girlfriend's skin (dots about the size of a fingernail). The sores seemed to have been burnt, almost as if her skin was melting.

As for the things that had taken up residence under my bed, I believe those were idols that the demonic powers had built. The little ones were placed in front of the big ones, and they wore crowns. To this very day, I can see them in my mind, and they are nothing to me, for I have Jesus Christ in my heart. I always ask Him to wrap me in His robe because I know what is out there. If I am wrapped in His robe, then I am safe.

All of these answers are real, but they only point to the *greatest answer*—JESUS CHRIST. He is the one who got ahold of me and saved me, completely changing my life. Still to this day, I am happy knowing that if sin comes into my mind, I can rebuke Satan in the name of Jesus Christ. I tell him to get behind me, for there is nothing that he tells me that I want to hear and nothing that he shows me that I want to see. Christ is my Savior, and the devil is nothing to me! I thank Jesus for giving me strength in Him and that just the sound of His name makes Satan tremble. I call upon His name when I need help. His is the most beautiful name in the world and the most powerful—*Jesus Christ*—because He is the ultimate answer, the truth, the light, and the best shepherd to us, His own sheep!

EPILOGUE

S o I ask you: Do you know the truth, the light? Or are you scared of the truth? Maybe you are running from the truth because if you are, Satan has you fooled. He is a liar—the king of lies and destruction. He has covered your eyes with a blindfold in the dark. Anything that he can say or do to blind you from Jesus Christ, he will do. This I have seen is real.

But Jesus has been given the crown of authority over all things, including Satan. God is our Father, the Creator of all things. Jesus Christ, His Son, died on the cross for every one of us. The Holy Spirit is there to help us make the right decisions. I am one of His many children. The problem is that there are many of His children who don't know Him or want to accept Him.

I ask you today, right now, even if you have already done it, confess to God that you are a sinner and that you believe that Jesus, the Christ, died on the cross for you. I ask you that when you read this, did you think, *I don't have to, I already did this?* Or did you think everything's okay, or even that I'm crazy? Now I ask you: think and pay close attention to what you thought and why you thought it because *are you being blinded?*

Can you confess to God too many times? The answer is, "No, we cannot," because God is God. He sent His only Son in flesh and blood to save those who believe and accept the gift of life after death, just as Jesus was raised to life after death. Because of that, I pray too that you will meet me at the greatest place ever—heaven!

So I ask, if you're not sure or never have found Him, then I seriously say, as a friend, someone who really loves you: have you confessed that you are a sinner, and have you asked Jesus to come into your heart? If you did, He will let you know by whatever means possible. Is He speaking to you right now?

God, I pray to You as I am of flesh and blood, a sinner. I ask that You please help the one who reads this that they too may find the answer that You have given us, Jesus Christ! For Jesus is the reason. You sent Him to teach us the truth, that He is the answer and the only answer. Christ is the only way to heaven for He is the way, the truth, and the life (John 14:6)! Amen.

NOTE

All names have been changed, except for those individuals listed in the introduction.

CONTACT

If you would like to correspond with the author, please e-mail: Rmoore4God@gmail.com

END

ABOUT THE AUTHOR

My name is Robert Moore IV, and I am soon to be fifty-four. I am a recovering addict. I have fought my demons for years and still as of today and will always fight my demons. I have been in and out of jail. I have stolen from my family. I have lost custody of my three beautiful children. Drugs have ruined my life, yet I made the choice to continue on the same path day after day. It wasn't until I allowed God to intervene that my life changed. God has spoken to me verbally starting in jail. As Jesus Christ is now my Savior that I truly found happiness and peace. I am here today to tell my story and answer questions as dark as they may be. In hope that it may offer hope to others who have and are battling demons and give the people an idea of what they are dealing with, seeing, and hearing while on drugs.

I can do all things through Christ who strengthens me.
—Philippians 4:13 (KJV)

CPSIA information can be obtained
at www.ICGtesting.com
Printed in the USA
BVHW051455270622
640741BV00003B/86

9 781638 602743